The Coppers' Lot...

To Jon,

Its good to know that even something as large as the Atlantic, can't get in the way of a strong friendship.

Best Wishes.

Paul McVeigh

March '23

The
Coppers' Lot...

Front Line Policing
in the UK

Rob Hindley

Rob Hindley February 2023

Matador
Unit E2 Airfield Business Park,
Harrison Road, Market Harborough,
Leicestershire. LE16 7UL
Tel: 0116 2792299
Email: books@troubador.co.uk
Web: www.troubador.co.uk/matador
Twitter: @matadorbooks

ISBN 9781 80313 5823

British Library Cataloguing in Publication Data.
A catalogue record for this book is available from the British Library.

Printed and bound by CPI Group (UK) Ltd, Croydon, CR0 4YY
Typeset in 11pt Minion Pro by Troubador Publishing Ltd, Leicester, UK

Matador is an imprint of Troubador Publishing Ltd

I am eternally grateful to my long-suffering wife Jenny and my daughter Florence for their love, support, and inspiration. I also want to express my thanks to my dear mother-in-law Sue as without her reading the drafts and offering her advice this book would not have reached this stage. Finally, I would like to express my gratitude to Marc Aldred-Young for designing the cover for the book.

"The darkest places in hell are reserved for those who maintain their neutrality in times of moral crisis…"

Dante Alighieri

Blessed are the peacemakers, for they will be called the children of God…

Mathew 5:9

CONTENTS

Preface   xi

PC Leon McLeod QGM (British Transport Police)   1

What is PTSD?   14

PC Kate Happe (Metropolitan Police)   17

PC Fiona Bone (Greater Manchester Police)   29

Violence Against the Police   41

Sergeant "David" (Greater Manchester Police)   44

Ill-Health Retirement   59

PC Richard Huber (South Yorkshire Police)   62

PC Jonathan Nicholas (Nottinghamshire Police)   76

Sergeant "Anna" (Midlands)   90

PC Paul McVeigh (Northumbria Police)   103

Trial by the Media   121

PC "Sarah" (West Country, England)   126

PC Darren Atkins (Metropolitan Police)   139

Police Suicide   151

PC Sam Smith (Hertfordshire Constabulary)   153

Conclusion   164

Endnotes   171

PREFACE

Policing is a uniquely dangerous, harrowing, and challenging profession in which officers are expected to do far more than prevent and detect crime. To be a police officer is also to be a social worker, a marriage guidance counsellor, a mental health worker and a medic. There has never been a harder time to be a police officer in the UK as they are underpaid and overworked while facing unprecedented levels of violence and trauma. However, day in and day out, the police go above and beyond what is required to protect and serve the public. In doing so they sacrifice a great deal of who they are, both mentally and physically.

In this book I will look at what motivates someone to join the police. What is it that the police really do? And how that work ultimately takes a huge toll on the officer's mental and physical health? The reader will be taken onto the front line of policing, dispelling the unrealistic and often biased media and entertainment depictions of officers.

The officers who contributed to this book have chosen to share their deeply personal experiences so that the reality of policing is exposed. They have all demonstrated the most incredible honesty and personal resilience, and each of them has my utmost respect and gratitude. Without their sacrifices and those of the thousands of other police officers around the country, we would not live as peacefully and safely as we do.

PC LEON MCLEOD QGM

(BRITISH TRANSPORT POLICE)

The terror attack that took place at Borough Market on the 3rd of June 2017 was the third act of terror in less than four months.

The first took place on the 22nd of March, when a lone terrorist driving a rented Hyundai Tucson mounted the pavement on Westminster Bridge. The driver accelerated to seventy-seven miles per hour before mowing down pedestrians, killing four and injuring at least fifty. He then crashed into security railings surrounding the Palace of Westminster, the heart of British democracy, getting out of the car he ran around the corner and into Carriage Gate, where he was tackled by PC Keith Palmer, who was unarmed. In the struggle that followed PC Palmer was stabbed twice before the terrorist was shot and killed by a ministerial close protection officer. Heroic passers-by including Conservative MP Tobias Ellwood attempted to save PC Palmer's life. Perversely, the acting commissioner of the Metropolitan Police and the highest-ranking police officer in the UK, watched the events unfold from inside his locked, chauffeur-driven BMW and did nothing to assist his fallen colleague. His actions were in complete contrast to the heroism demonstrated by PC Palmer, who was posthumously awarded the George Medal for his actions.

Two months later, on the 22nd of May in the city of Manchester, a suicide bomber detonated his device as people began to leave an Ariana Grande concert. Twenty-two people were killed, the youngest just nine years old, and more than a hundred people, including many children, were injured.

Within two weeks on the 3rd of June, there was a further terror attack. This one took place in Borough Market in the heart of London. As in the Westminster attack the terrorists used a vehicle to mount the pavement as they crossed London Bridge mowing down pedestrians. The van they were using drove off the bridge onto Borough High Street, where it continued to target pedestrians before crashing near the Barrow Boy & Banker pub. The three terrorists abandoned the van, which was loaded with petrol bombs, and ran towards Borough Market. Each was armed with a ceramic knife taped to his wrist and each was wearing what appeared to be a suicide vest. Although Borough Market has several restaurants and pubs, it is usually a quiet area that traditionally caters for commuters during the week. However, on that Saturday it was busier than usual as the final of the UEFA Champions League, between Juventus and Real Madrid, had been screened live in the nearby pubs and bars.

As the attack began to unfold, just a short distance away PCs Leon McLeod and Wayne Marques of the British Transport Police (BTP) were leaving the rear yard of the London Bridge Police Station to go on patrol. The officers had been in the same intake at training school and had only been operational for fourteen months. Leon said, "As soon as we left the station yard, I heard a noise. It's weird, though, as I still can't say what it was. Maybe a kind of bang or something, but it didn't worry me. We were looking down towards Borough Market but couldn't see anything. We were about to move on when Wayne stopped again and said, 'I think that there's a fight'."

What follows is Leon's account of what happened next.

2

"We had run about fifty yards when people started running towards us, they were pointing and saying, 'They've gone that way.' As we moved forward, I saw a bloke face down on the floor. A member of the public was applying pressure to a stab wound in his back. I didn't have time to react as I heard a noise from my right. I looked over to see Wayne was outnumbered and backing away from people trying to fight with him. As the casualty was already being treated, I went to assist Wayne. As I got to him, I realised that he was reaching for his baton. I knew then that this was serious as Wayne can usually deal with anything and he very rarely uses his baton. As I started to take it all in, I saw that the guy had a knife in his hand. He was only a few yards away from us and we were in danger of being seriously hurt or killed. I thought to myself, *well this is different*; all my focus was on the guy with the knife, though I knew he was not on his own.

"The knifeman didn't move, didn't run, he just stood there. Then I heard someone else say, 'Run away!' As they ran it was as if my tunnel vision had widened, and now I was aware that there were two other casualties: a woman, and another man who was holding a skateboard to his chest. I got on my radio to update the control room about everything that was happening and to request more ambulances. I was monitoring the casualties when the man with the skateboard died. I saw the precise moment that the life left his eyes and the skateboard he had been holding slowly rolled away. It was such a weird experience. I felt awful because there was absolutely nothing that I could do to help him. I found out later that his name was Ignacio Echeverria.

"I knew that I needed to find the people who'd done this and stop them killing or injuring anyone else. As I began looking for the attackers, Wayne reappeared. His head was covered in blood, and he was limping. I wasn't concerned initially as head wounds always bleed, and as for the limp, I knew he had a dodgy hip or something. I got him to sit down and started passing more updates over my radio. That's when a detective joined us, and although I recognised him, I didn't know him. I later found out that his name was Alfred. As he started to help Wayne, I moved off again, searching for the attackers. I was still oblivious to the fact that it was a marauding terror attack. I just hadn't had time to process anything. I do remember that suddenly it felt really dark, and the streets were not as busy as before.

"As I was trying to track down the attackers, I kept finding more and more casualties. I remember saying over the radio that this was an extremely serious situation. However, I still didn't want to say it was a terror attack as I thought it would set a lot of people panicking. I was doing a triage thing: *What have I got? Are they being helped? And is there anything I can do that isn't already being done?* When I was satisfied that there wasn't, I would move on, still looking for the perpetrators. At one point I saw Met units were arriving, so I flagged one down and gave the officer a full update just in case all the details weren't being passed across their radio channels.

"When I came to Bedale Street near the corner of Borough Market I found two more people who had been stabbed. Then an off-duty soldier came up to me and asked, 'Is this what I think it is?' I said, 'Yeah it is', and then I told him to help me. We were trying to treat a guy lying next to a car when I saw the Met firearms officers arriving. I realised that we had no hard cover, so we moved the guy we were treating to a safer place. I don't know how we did it, but we moved him up towards London Bridge. I then heard three quick gunshots; I think there were more but I'm not sure. It's weird because I never felt scared even with all the people being stabbed and shot all over the place.

"When I got onto London Bridge, I saw the van that had been used in the attack for the first time. At the time, though, I wondered if someone passing had panicked and crashed. It was then that I saw Wayne again and now he didn't look good at all. He

4

was being treated by a first responder medic and Alfred. The first responder grabbed me and said, 'You have got to get him out of here! He needs to be in hospital urgently! I had only seen Wayne a few minutes before and couldn't understand what had gone wrong so quickly. With the help of a member of the public we carried him further onto London Bridge. Even at the time I remember being impressed by the fact that people were helping us; I was thinking that it was such a decent thing to be doing. Fortunately, we came across a load of BTP officers who took over. It wasn't until later that I found out that Wayne was taken to hospital in the back of a police van. On the way Alfred had searched Wayne's pockets to see if there was anything in them that could have hurt him. In doing so he discovered that they were full of blood and that Wayne had been stabbed in the upper thigh.

"In the meantime, I went back to help the first responder as I knew there were still loads of casualties who needed to be moved out of the hot zone, as obviously nobody else would be allowed in until it was safe. Over the radio I could hear various colleagues calling for first-aid kits and I was hoping that the medic was going to be able to help as I knew our bog-standard kits were not going to be enough.

"Around this time, I took a minute to check the time on my phone. It was weird because it felt like everything had been going on for hours, but it was only about 10.30 and I sent a quick message to my partner, just letting her know I was alright. I knew she would worry if she found out what was going on. She was at home alone with our baby son who was eighteen months old. I then had to stop thinking about them and get on with my job. At the time there was still so much confusion about what was going on. We knew by then that three terrorists had been shot dead but there was still a belief that there was a fourth one out there somewhere.

"I was then told to join a makeshift 'serial' and we were tasked with evacuating people who were still locked in the pubs and restaurants. While doing this I could see casualties all over the place; most were being treated by ambulance crews. It felt weird to see the extent of the violence that had occurred in such a short space of time. Personally, I still felt that there was more that I could do to help, and I didn't want to be pulled out early. Fortunately, when the sergeant leading us realised that I had been dealing with the incident from the beginning, he didn't overreact. He was brilliant: he made sure that I was okay and fit to work, and then he let me get on with it without fussing over me.

"At around 2.30 in the morning our serial was pulled out of the scene and was ordered to go to the police office at Waterloo Train Station. Although I was happy to be pulled out with the other officers it was weird because I didn't travel with them. I ended up being taken back in a car on my own. I think that's when the magnitude of what had happened really hit me for the first time; I was struggling to hold back the tears. When I got there a friend came over and asked, 'Are you alight?' and then I completely lost it and broke down; I was a mess of emotions. Someone put me in a quiet room so that I had some headspace. It was weird because I didn't really know what I was crying for; I guess it was just a way of releasing the tension. A detective came and sat with me. She was brilliant: she was really caring, but she also made me laugh.

"Before she could record my first account, the deputy chief constable came in to see me. I had met him a few times before and knew that he was a nice guy with a human side, which made him different to a lot of senior officers. The first thing he said to me was that Wayne had asked how I was. That set me off again because I had been worrying about how he was getting on. It was a relief when I was told that he was stable. We then went upstairs; we were looking for a quiet room so that she could take my statement. I then saw one of the PCSOs on my team. I knew he would have been out in Borough Market when the attack happened. He was in tears, so I gave him a hug. That's when I saw the PCSO he had been working with. The poor man's lip was quivering, so I hugged him too.

"While we were walking around, I had this weird feeling that people were staring at me, even though I am sure they probably weren't. I suppose it could have just been because of all the blood on my uniform but it wasn't until we were in an office that I realised just how much there really was. It wasn't just on my yellow jacket I could even see it on my black trousers. Later, after the detective had seized my uniform for forensic testing, I found that the blood had soaked through and stained my legs. I ended up in an oversized custody tracksuit usually reserved for prisoners. It was weird to see that there were loads of other cops were wearing them too.

"We eventually finished at about five or six in the morning. As I had driven into work the night before I really didn't want to leave my car behind; the problem was, everyone was worried about me driving home. In the end it was agreed that it would be okay. I was taken back to London Bridge and allowed to go through the cordon to the station. I changed into my own clothes and made a coffee. I then decided that I needed to update my pocket notebook before I left work, I don't know why, but I just didn't want to get bollocked when I next went on duty for not having it up to date."

The sustained bravery that Leon displayed throughout that night is awe-inspiring. He had watched a man die and had been in no doubt that he too was in mortal danger. However, he continued to track the attackers around the market, moving from one scene of carnage to the next. Each time his priority was to save people's lives and his courage, compassion and professionalism never waned.

He continued, "Driving home, I tried to listen to a podcast as a bit of a distraction, but as I got closer, I started getting really upset again. I don't ever talk about work at home, but I knew that this was different, and I needed to talk about what had just happened. It almost seemed like my partner was waiting behind the door for me. When I was inside, I said, 'Do you want to know what happened?'

Fortunately, she did, and we talked it through. I knew I needed to get some sleep but I was worried that I would just have nightmares and flashbacks. I also couldn't stop thinking about Ignacio and how his skateboard had rolled away when he died. I knew that if anything got to me it would be that. It was like something from a horror film. When I did get to bed, I thought about him and about everything that had happened throughout the night. I was lucky as I got a few hours of undisturbed sleep."

Sunday was an incredibly hard day for Leon. He said, "I was very tired and drained. I was also emotional and almost anything would set me off." He tried to slowly work his way through all the messages he had received from friends and family during the night: "I wanted to let everyone know that I was okay, but I didn't want to go into any detail about what had happened." After putting a blanket post on social media, he turned off his phone to get some space away from the incident. He spent the rest of the day trying to be normal, doing ordinary things like bathing his baby son.

Although Leon had been scheduled to work Sunday night he had been told to stay at home. He was exhausted and decided to try and have an early night. However, he was still anxious that his sleep would be disturbed by nightmares. Before trying to sleep, he again thought through the incident and about the death of Ignacio. "I don't know if actively thinking about it meant that it wasn't in my subconscious, but thinking things through did initially help me to sleep undisturbed for a few hours at a time during the first couple of weeks."

On Monday, less than forty-eight hours after the attack, Leon went back to work. He said, "I needed to order a new dress uniform and I wanted to be around my mates for a couple of hours. I should have been on nights anyway, so I didn't mind." His first proper day back at work was Thursday, just five days after the attack. "I had to cobble a uniform together using my spare body armour which was uncomfortable. I ended up working with a colleague who I had known since we'd played junior football together as kids. It was a difficult day. I still randomly wanted to cry. We didn't do much: just a couple of short foot patrols around the market area, I don't know why but I needed to see it again."

In the days after the attack, the media constantly reported the story on every available platform. For the officers and members of the public who were present at the scene of an attack this can have a negative psychological impact as each report can cause them to mentally relive the trauma. It was frustrating, too, that what was reported about the Borough Market attack was often wrong. Can you imagine just popping into a local shop for a pint of milk and seeing your face all over the front pages? The very thought of it would disturb most of us. However, for Leon this was a regular trigger which drew him back into the most horrific moments of his life, and consequently had an impact on him coming to terms with what had happened. Then on the 14th of June a massive fire broke out at Grenfell Tower, a high-rise residential block of flats, and claimed seventy-two lives. As the media now had a new story to sensationalise and exploit, reporting on Borough Market virtually ceased. Despite the tragedy of the fire, Leon was relieved to now have some respite from the unrelenting media attention.

Leon is a very easy-going man who enjoys the "banter and piss-taking" which usually underpin a close-knit police team. However, as the weeks rolled into months, he began to realise that he was not himself. Nonetheless, he was sure that it would eventually pass, and he would be back to his normal self. In the meantime, he would put on an act to reassure others that he was fine. His jokes were becoming forced, and he would question himself afterwards: what are you doing Leon? Why did you say that? Things at home were no better and his relationship was under increasing pressure: "Despite having a wife and a one-year-old boy who I loved more than anything in the world, I would still go out and get drunk, even on my own. That was never part of my character before the attack."

In the months leading up to Christmas he had partially moved out of the family home and was staying at his parents' house. As a devoted dad, he moved between the two to be there for his little boy. Soon after, his marriage ended, and his wife moved away.

Leon said, "I know now that I was suffering with Post Traumatic Stress Disorder (PTSD) and anxiety. I was self-medicating with alcohol, which doesn't work and might be why I was having suicidal thoughts." However, as it was now the festive period, he convinced himself that his drinking was normal, after all, everyone drinks more at this time of the year. Nevertheless, when it came to the crunch, he knew that he was struggling to cope so he began to look around for help by contacting various police welfare charities before finally finding an organisation called PTSD999.

In the new year he began to see a counsellor, however, after several sessions he knew that the counsellor was not the right person to help him, and he began to work with someone else. "The hardest part when you begin therapy is talking about your problems, but with time you come up with coping mechanisms. It might feel difficult, but you need to be honest with your closest friends and family, as they are the people who know you best and ultimately want what is best for you."

While in therapy he came to realise that he was no longer doing the things that had previously given him pleasure. One of those things was running, he used to regularly do 5K runs to keep fit. "I decided to get back into it, which was good as I also started to reduce the amount that I was drinking. I really got back into running, and it started to make me feel better." He added, "I had this idea that I wanted to raise some money for charity, and it had always been on my bucket list to run a marathon, so I decided that I would challenge myself and combine the two. I was really motivated to do the marathon so that I could raise some money for PTSD999. The only issue was that I had missed the cut-off date to enter the race. It was a bit cheeky, but I called the race organisers and explained who I was and what I wanted to do. They were amazing and made an exception that allowed me to take part. I had set a target to raise £1,000, and in the end, I raised a bit more than that."

Completing the marathon was a significant turning point for Leon. He was now spending more time with his friends and family, he was fitter than he had been, and self-medicating with alcohol was no longer an issue. "For me, it's about being healthy and now I can socialise without drinking." Leon continues to be a devoted, loving father who sees his son as often as possible. "I am getting used to renting Airbnbs on my rest days so that I can be near him." Although the PTSD will never go away, he now recognises the symptoms and triggers and is able to manage them with the techniques learned in therapy. As for work, "I'm still a police officer it might sound bizarre, but I love the job and my colleagues have been so supportive through everything."

The death of Ignacio Echeverria is a profound memory for Leon, so who was this hero who gave his life to save the lives of others? Ignacio was a thirty-nine-year-old Spaniard who had been living in London since 2015. An extremely intelligent man, he was fluent in English, French and German and had law degrees from both Spain and France. Before moving to London, he worked as a lawyer in Spain, earning the nickname "Abo" among his skating friends (*abogado* being the Spanish word for lawyer) it was a nickname that he had for the rest of his life, despite the fact he had moved away from Law when he became an anti-money-laundering specialist, first at a bank in Spain.

This was short-lived as he discovered that the bank was accepting illegal transactions and he stood up to the board of directors forcing them to take responsibility before he was fired. His sister Isabel said, "He was a very principled man and always stood up for what he believed, even when he knew that it would have a negative effect on his career." Having been fired he moved to London. Ignacio loved the city and soon he was soon offered a job with one of the world's leading banks.

His principles came from his upbringing in the suburbs of Madrid. His parents are devout Catholics who had brought their children up to be principled enough to stand up for those who needed help and support. Ignacio would exemplify those values as he often went out of his way to protect people. In one example, he was surfing one day when he noticed an elderly couple struggling to stay afloat in the waves. Without hesitation he passed his surfboard to a friend before swimming out to the couple and pulling them back to the safety of the beach.

Although he enjoyed many sports his passion was for skateboarding which he took up as a young boy. When he wasn't at work, he immersed himself in the skateboard scene where he quickly made friends. Isabel fondly describes him as "the oldest skater by far." In another example of his courage, Ignacio was at a skatepark one day when he saw a teenage boy harassing a younger girl. He stepped in and told the boy to leave, however, the next day the boy returned with his older brother, and he was badly beaten up. Isabel said, "Ignacio didn't regret getting involved, it's who he was, he would never just turn a blind eye."

On the day of the attack Ignacio had been skating with friends before they arrived at Borough Market just after ten. He then saw a woman on the floor, she was being stabbed by a man. With no concern for his personal safety, he intervened and repeatedly hit the man with his skateboard, however, while trying to save her life he was stabbed by another of the terrorists. The woman would survive the attack and I'm sure that his heroic intervention made all the difference. The loss of Ignacio devastated his close family, tragically their pain was made worse as his death was not confirmed for five days. During that time Isabel searched the hospitals never knowing if he was alive or dead.

For his incredible bravery Ignacio was posthumously awarded the George Medal, which was handed to his family by Her Majesty the Queen at Buckingham Palace; a small consolation to a family who had lost so much. In Spain he was celebrated with several awards including the Grand Cross of the Order of Civil Merit. Of all the awards he received, the one that would have meant the most to him was the creation of a skatepark near his family home which is dedicated to him. Isabel said, "Sometimes we can hear the noise of the skaters and it always reminds me of Ignacio."

Leon and Wayne were also recognised for their bravery. For his efforts, Leon was awarded the prestigious Queen's Gallantry Medal (QGM). "It was weird being at the palace, waiting to meet the Queen. I'm just a normal guy who had grown up in South London. It was so weird, I kept wondering how someone like me could end up there. I was proud to meet Ignacio's family and I would have spoken to them more, except the language barrier made it difficult. When I did get called to meet the Queen, I was impressed that she had been standing all day and that she knew who we all were and a little about what we had done."

Although the attack at Borough Market was the most horrific incident of his life, Leon remains positive and still sees the good in people. He recognises the selfless courage of his colleagues and the civilians who stood up against evil. In recognition of that, he commissioned a tattoo above his knee. It depicts a London landscape, below which are the following lyrics from one of his favourite artists:

See that is London and that is Britain
We might get scratched, and we might get bitten
But when our heart and resolve is depleted
We won't lay down no, we won't be defeated.

13

WHAT IS PTSD?

This overview of PTSD is not exhaustive or clinically based and is only intended to give a general understanding of the condition. First PTSD is the normal reaction to abnormal circumstances; human beings are not able to withstand exposure to severe, repeated trauma. It's estimated that most people are exposed to extreme trauma on three to four occasions during their lives. However, during a police career, officers can be exposed to extreme trauma on four to six *hundred* occasions. It is little wonder, therefore, that research carried out by Dr Jess Miller has established that one in five officers are suffering with PTSD or complex PTSD (C-PTSD).

So, what are the four main groups of PTSD symptoms?

1. Reliving the traumatic event, perhaps in the form of flashbacks, nightmares or intrusive memories which can be terrifying as the person is reliving the event.
2. Avoiding situations that remind the person of the event.
3. Negative changes in beliefs and feelings.
4. Feeling hypervigilant and fearful of people and the world around them (also called "hyperarousal".

CPTSD is usually a result of repeated or sustained traumas and presents in a similar way to PTSD, but with some additional symptoms. I have not listed these in any order of relevance; however, these may also include:

- Disruptions to the person's daily routine.
- Severe distress and intense fear when triggered.
- Difficulty in controlling emotions.
- Irritability and/or anger.
- Trouble sleeping.
- Periods of losing attention and concentration (dissociation).
- General memory problems.
- Physical symptoms such as headaches, dizziness, chest pains and stomach aches.
- Isolation from friends and family, or neglecting or abandoning activities formally enjoyed.
- Feeling detached from others, including relationship difficulties.
- Self-destructive or risky behaviour such as self-harm, alcohol misuse or drug abuse.
- Feeling hopeless about the future.
- Overwhelming feelings of shame or guilt.
- Suicidal thoughts.

The brain is hardwired with a fight-or-flight reflex triggered when we perceive a threat or danger. When triggered the body releases cortisol, epinephrine, and norepinephrine, which activate the nervous system, initiating a physiological response that speeds up respiration, constricts blood vessels, dilates the pupils, and slows down the digestive system; this allows muscles to react powerfully and faster. Essential when deciding whether to stand and fight or run away. For the police the option of running away must be suppressed as they are required to take decisive action to avert any threat of harm to the public. As policing is incredibly unpredictable, officers must develop a heightened sense of awareness as they literally don't know what's around the next corner. Essentially, they live their lives in a state of hypervigilance. For an officer who is suffering with PTSD (diagnosed or not) they are likely to develop CPTSD as they will continue to deal with traumatic incidents resulting in serious long-term effects on their personal life and mental health.

Unfortunately, there is still a stigma attached to mental health issues in the police and consequently it prevents officers who are ill from asking for help when they need it, leaving them to cope on their own. For those who are brave enough to ask for it, they are often let down as the forces do not have a properly funded occupational health unit to offer any meaningful treatment. As such they are referred to the NHS where long waiting lists can mean that the officer will be off work long term. This causes further stress as the officer is pressured into returning to work without having any treatment, both by supervisors and the financial implications of dropping to half pay after six months or zero pay after twelve.

The stigma also means that many of these officers are treated with suspicion and are often perceived to be weak or lazy. Therefore, on their return they don't get the support that they need. Having spoken to many hundreds of officers they regularly report that when they go back to work, they are placed on a "return to work plan" which outlines expectations that are almost impossible to meet. A frequent example is that the officer should not go off sick again during the next year. When officers fail to meet these expectations, they then find themselves being placed on Unsatisfactory Performance Procedures (UUP) which can ultimately lead to them being dismissed from the force which is scandalous.

PC KATE HAPPE
(METROPOLITAN POLICE)

When Kate joined the police at twenty years old, she was following in the footsteps of both her grandfather and her father, both having long and successful careers. Her grandfather had joined following his service with the Royal Navy, retiring twenty-five years later as a sergeant. Her father served for thirty years, retiring as an inspector.

Having grown up around police officers, Kate always had an interest in the job; in fact, she fondly remembers being taken out in the back of a police car by her father on several occasions when she was young. "In those days you would be able to get away with it," she reflected. At thirteen, the children at her school had the opportunity to do some work experience. Although the police had offered several placements they were all filled very quickly. Undeterred, Kate did her work experience at a local dairy farm: "I absolutely loved it. I loved being outside all day, caring for the cows and getting stuck into everything else that was required to run the farm." In fact, her time at the farm went so well that she was offered a Saturday job and over the years she learned all the aspects of being a 'herdsman'. She joked, "The first vehicle I ever drove was a tractor. I knew quite quickly that this was what I wanted to do with my life." After leaving school she went on to study for a National Diploma in animal care.

It may have seemed an unusual career path for a young woman who had grown up in the suburbs of one of the biggest and most cosmopolitan cities in the world; however, Kate's love for animals and the great outdoors made her perfectly suited to the role. Unfortunately, her dreams were dashed following the outbreak of bovine spongiform encephalopathy (BSE), or 'mad cow disease', as it was more commonly known. At the peak of the outbreak over four million cattle were destroyed and 178 people died after catching the human variant, Creutzfeldt-Jakob disease (CJD). The industry was left devastated. Kate said, "When they started selling cows at market for, like, a fiver, I knew I wouldn't be able to make a living any longer, so I had a rethink of my career options and decided I'd join the police."

When she talked to her dad, he advised her to get a little more life experience before applying. Taking his advice, Kate decided to apply for a civilian job as a criminal justice unit (CJU) case clerk. "I hated being stuck inside behind a desk and I hated the monotony of admin work." However, there was a silver lining. "I was taken out in police cars on a couple of night duties, gaining experience of what a police officer does. I even met some officers from the dog unit. I asked if I could come out on a day's attachment with them whenever I could. I did all the attachments in my own time. That was it, then: I was completely hooked, and all I wanted to do was become a dog handler."

After sticking it out as a CJU clerk for eighteen long, tedious months, she was successful in her application to become a police officer and began her recruit training in January 2001. She had prepared herself for everything that the training would have to offer. "I was a fit twenty-one-year-old who had never had any previous illnesses or injuries." Reflecting on her civilian role, she added, "The experience came in handy as I was able to teach my class how to complete case papers for court." Kate excelled at the training centre, and when she passed all her exams, she was posted to a response team working out of Wood Green Police Station in the borough of Haringey. She didn't know the area very well, having only gone there as a teenager to ice-skate or to watch her favourite team Tottenham Hotspur play.

Kate's enthusiasm and outgoing personality meant that she quickly became a well-loved member of her team. She thrived on the adrenalin and diversity of response policing and worked extremely hard, trying to take on as many challenges as she could so that her experience and skills would improve. Twenty-two months in, she was nearing the end of her two-year probationary period and still had her heart set on a transfer to the dog section after her probation was complete. She was happy, and life was panning out just the way she wanted it to, she was also in a relationship with a colleague, Ian, and they were looking to move into a new flat within the next few days.

Kate said, "Looking back I now believe that I had a sixth sense about what was going to happen on the night of the 26th of November 2002. It should have been just another shift; I had done hundreds of them and felt confident in my abilities. However, I remember getting into my uniform and looking at my underwear and wondering if it looked okay. I remember thinking, *who cares what I'm wearing? Nobody is going to see it!* I also had a load of empty cigarette boxes in the bottom of my locker, and thought that I should clear them out in case Ian needed to get into it, as he hated me smoking. It was such an odd thought as there was no reason for him to go into it.

"On parade, the sergeant went through the duties for the night, he had changed mine and I was posted to work with a different officer. I was immediately worried about working with him as his driving had scared me in the past; I felt he drove way too quickly. The police car we ended up taking out was the only one that didn't have a 'black box' so I was worried about what would happen if something went wrong; nobody would know what speed we were doing or how he was driving. I considered speaking to the sergeant about my concerns but then I thought to myself, *you've only got twenty-two months in the job, and they'll just tell you to shut up and get on with it."*

In the early hours of the morning Kate and her colleague were back at Wood Green Police Station having their meal break when a call came over the radio about a possible burglary at a builder's merchant's. "We abandoned our dinner and turned out to back up other officers already heading there. It was a big site, and we would need quite a few officers to contain it properly." Kate and her colleague left the station, followed by a second police car. She was apprehensive as her colleague accelerated. The roads were quiet, and he was soon travelling at high speed. Devastatingly, her worst fears were justified when they were travelling along White Hart Lane and the driver lost control of the vehicle, which spun before careening off the road and slamming into a tree at an estimated seventy-three miles per hour. The force of the impact was so great that the car was effectively torn apart. The police car travelling behind them to the emergency call immediately stopped. The passenger, got out to help while the driver turned back and drove to a local fire station. Despite the fire service being on a national strike, they did not hesitate to abandon their picket line to assist.

At the same time, Ian and his colleague were in a takeaway, waiting for their food. He said, "It came over the radio that a police car had crashed. This can happen and it's usually minor, so at first, I wasn't particularly concerned so we decided to wait for our meal. It must have been seconds before the officer on scene was back on the radio, requesting that all officers attend the scene and bring their fire extinguishers as the crashed vehicle was beginning to smoke. I knew then that it was obviously very serious. I didn't know that it was Kate's car that had crashed, and as we approached, I was shocked by the severity of the damage. I ran to the passenger side and saw Kate slumped in the seat, moaning in pain. I couldn't see the driver at first but then realised he had been severely injured, and his head was part way out of the open rear driver's-side door, and he was being treated by another officer. I got into the car behind Kate and held her head steady until the paramedics and firefighters arrived."

Kate recalled, "The firefighters realised how serious my condition was, so instead of cutting me out of the car they just dragged me out. It was life or death and any risk to me was outweighed by me dying if I didn't reach the hospital quickly. As soon as they put me on the stretcher I apparently started choking and coughing up blood. I hadn't done that in the car as I'd been sitting up. I'm incredibly lucky that a doctor had been out that night with the advanced paramedic and was able to provide immediate treatment. I was then loaded into the ambulance."

Ian added, "While the doctor and two paramedics were treating Kate in the back of the ambulance, I was up front as we travelled to the North Middlesex Hospital. As soon as she arrived at the hospital she was rushed straight into resus. I had to stay in the waiting room on my own until other officers arrived. I had no idea what was happening to her. While there, I saw the girlfriend of Kate's colleague arrive. She was quickly ushered out of the waiting room and down a corridor. Soon after I heard her piercing scream, which just confirmed how bad the situation really was.

"Just sitting in the waiting room was horrendous and I needed something to do to distract me. Although I don't smoke, I went outside with a colleague who wanted to have a cigarette. When we got outside the hospital, I saw a chief inspector who I didn't recognise making a phone call. I heard him say that one officer was dead and the other was unlikely to survive." It was a horrible way for Ian to find out that Kate's life was in the balance, particularly as he had not heard anything official from the doctors. Despite being completely shell-shocked by the news he held it together so that he could be close to Kate.

During the next few long hours, the doctors fought desperately to keep Kate alive. All the time, Ian waited anxiously for news. He had been joined by Kate's mum, Alison, and they provided some support to each other. Throughout that time Kate suffered two cardiac arrests and came close to losing her life. It would be twelve hours before she was stable enough for Ian and Alison to get their first chance to see her. Later she was moved from resus into the intensive care unit. Ian went with her and slept in the waiting room outside. Finally, when the full extent of Kate's injuries was revealed, it was devastating news. She had sustained a serious head injury, her pelvis was broken in eight places, she had four broken ribs (two either side of her chest), both lungs were punctured, and one of them had collapsed. She also had serious whiplash and a broken hand. Glass fragments covered her face. In the next couple of days Ian spent most of his time at the hospital, often with Alison, and they quickly became firm friends. It was an incredibly difficult period for them both as Kate was still in a critical condition. Three days after the accident Ian had to leave Kate and make their move to the new flat which they had been dreaming about. However, with her life still in the balance, there was very little to celebrate or look forward to.

In all, Kate would spend three weeks in intensive care before she was moved to an orthopaedic ward, where she would be treated for her physical injuries. However, the doctors were concerned about her recovery, suggesting that she might never be able to walk again. Although the ward staff were very kind and well intentioned, they were ill equipped to deal with the effects of Kate's traumatic head injury. It's unfortunately common for people who have suffered a serious brain injury to exhibit a range of emotional problems. In Kate's case she struggled with her emotions and could be irritable, confused, and short-tempered, and she swore repeatedly. As a result, she needed a great deal of additional care, and it was Alison and Ian who stepped in to provide it. Each morning Alison went to the hospital and gave Kate her breakfast and lunch, and stayed with her until Ian could take over. As he had to go back to work (he had been given a day job), after work he would relieve Alison and stay with Kate until visiting hours finished at around ten. Occasionally he would take Alison back home before returning to the hospital. As such, their friendship grew further, and they came to rely on each other emotionally. The head injury apart, Kate was beginning to make progress on the ward and her physical injuries began to improve. Then one night, out of the blue, she fell out of her hospital bed. Fearing the worst, the doctors rushed her to X-ray, concerned that she might have sustained further injury or – perish the thought – even worsened her existing ones. However, the opposite was true. To everyone's amazement, she was healing far quicker than the doctors had anticipated.

Remarkably, after just nine weeks in hospital Kate was allowed home. Leaving hospital was bittersweet as she could not move into the new flat that she and Ian had been so looking forward to, as she was unable to use the stairs and needed constant supervision and support. Instead, she and Ian went to live with her mother, who set up her front room as a bedroom for them. Alison remained on unpaid leave so that she could care for Kate during the day, and as they had done when she was in hospital, Ian took over in the evening. Unforgivably, nobody from the police had made any official contact with Kate or her family. It was Alison who was forced to contact them. She was concerned as Kate had now passed her two-year probation period and she was determined to ensure that she was confirmed in rank as a police constable.

Now, although Kate was making an amazing physical recovery, the same couldn't be said for her brain injury. She had to relearn how to do things that she had taken for granted in the past, and this was extremely hard. She credits Ian and her loved ones for the love and patience they showed in supporting her to move slowly forward. Following a couple of stays at the police rehabilitation centre, someone suggested that she needed to be seen by a counsellor to deal with the trauma of the accident. The force arranged for her to see a man in occupational health. Unfortunately, he refused to deal with her as he couldn't handle her swearing and the side effects of her head injury. Therefore, she was forced to seek treatment on the NHS. As luck would have it, she saw someone after a short wait. Kate described the counsellor as a "lovely lady in her sixties." She added, "When I told her that I had been dropped by my last counsellor for swearing, she said that this was a normal symptom of a brain injury, and she made me swear all through the sessions. She was such a great help to me in the end."

After living with Alison for almost a year, Kate was strong enough to move into her own place with Ian. While living with Alison the couple had saved up for a deposit and could now buy a house. After such a long recovery they were optimistic about the future. At work Ian had moved out of his office-based job and was beginning to get his career back on track. Despite Kate still undergoing physical therapy, she had defied all expectations and returned to work in February 2004 in a recuperative role. However, she was forced to jump through ludicrous bureaucratic hoops. During her time off sick, she had accrued a substantial amount of leave. As a result, she was given an ultimatum: either she used it before she came back, or she would lose it. Reluctant to take more time off she had no choice but to lose it all.

While on recuperative duties Kate pushed herself hard, and it was only down to her sheer indomitable resilience that she was able to return to response policing in early 2005. She had worked incredibly hard to relearn the role and to rebuild herself physically. Returning to her original response team made things a little easier as she had friends waiting to welcome her back; however, the sergeants and inspector were all new as her previous supervisors had all moved on to other roles. This made it difficult for Kate as they didn't know or even understand everything that she had been through. Despite relearning so much she was aware that she would need support, especially as she was still so early in her service and had been away from frontline policing for a considerable time. She approached the sergeants explaining her concerns and asking to be paired up with an experienced officer for a few weeks while she found her feet.

She was relieved on her first day back when she was assigned to work with a couple of highly experienced officers. Shortly after going out on patrol, they were tasked to a disturbance at a local pub. On arrival they established that a drunk woman had smashed a window. Kate arrested her for criminal damage. Nervous and excited, she was glad to have her crewmates' support to ensure that she got through all the custody procedures and the prisoner interview which would have bolstered her confidence. However, when they reached custody, the sergeant ordered her crewmates to resume patrol and left Kate to deal with everything alone. She was completely overwhelmed, and it was only with the support and assistance of other colleagues in the custody block that she was able to muddle through the processes and get the woman charged. Her first day back at work was made extremely stressful and unnecessarily difficult, and unfortunately things were not about to get any better.

On the second day she tried again to speak to the sergeants. She hoped that maybe they had not properly understood what she needed. However, once again her request fell on deaf ears; in fact, within days of being back at work she was tasked with reporting a road traffic accident where another police officer had been seriously injured, exactly the type of incident likely to trigger memories of her own traumatic experience. Kate approached her sergeant and asked, "Do you really think it's appropriate for me to deal with this?" He replied simply, "Yes, of course I do; get on with it." A few days later she was posted to the front office of a smaller police station on a Sunday late shift. At that time there was nobody else in the building and she was left to deal with whatever came in on her own. The sad thing is that it was not just one of the sergeants who showed her very little support: there were three of them, and whatever she did, they came down on her hard.

For example, when the dog section advertised vacancies, she knew that she wasn't ready to apply but she wanted to submit "an expression of interest" so that they would be aware of her in the future. In response, she recalled, "One of the sergeants dragged me into the office where there was another sergeant waiting. He ripped into me, telling me that I was completely shit at my job and that he would never support an application for me to move. I tried to reason with him again by explaining why I needed some extra help. Whatever I tried to say to him, it was ignored. He just wasn't interested, and in the end, I got so upset that I threatened to resign. At that point he backtracked and said he wanted to resolve my complaints. In the end I was paired up on the odd occasion with an experienced officer. However, I never properly got the support I had asked for." Had Kate resigned, she would not have been able to claim constructive dismissal as police officers are office holders and not employees, and as such have very little protection under employment law.

Kate was due to work a night shift on the anniversary of her accident, although she didn't want to take the night off, she was anxious about how she would cope responding at high speed particularly on White Hart Lane. Fortunately, her duties showed her working away from the area. She spoke to the duties sergeant and confirmed that the duties would not be changed as she didn't feel she'd be able to cope if they did. However, when the night came, he had changed the duties and commented to her shift partner, "Best you don't drive down White Hart Lane", before giggling and walking away. This is exactly the type of callous behaviour that reinforces the stigma of mental health difficulties and prevents officers from safely asking for help when they urgently need it.

Kate would have been fully justified in raising a grievance for bullying against all three men, yet she didn't as she didn't want to rock the boat. Instead, she bravely endured the situation and relied on her incredible tenacity as she honed her skills and she again became the highly effective officer that she had once been. Although, to be fair she was always fully respected by her colleagues, it wasn't until the sergeants started to move on to other posts and were replaced by a couple of new female sergeants that things began to improve, and she was treated with a little more compassion and respect.

Undeterred by the unwarranted criticism and bullying, in 2007 Kate moved from response to the proactive priority crime team. This gave her a chance to gain even more operational experience, which would improve her prospects of joining the dog section. She enjoyed her new job and got on well with her new team and they soon made an impact in reducing gang crime in Haringey and were awarded with commendations. Finally, everything was looking good for the future.

Then in 2008 her dream was dashed once again. Kate was on duty when she was struggling to get a violent arrestee into the back of the police van. The prisoner slipped and fell forward, instinctively Kate tried to catch her, as she did so the woman kicked back, striking Kate in the centre of her chest, and forcing her shoulders upwards. As the days passed the pain in her shoulders increased; so much so that she was referred for surgery on them both, leaving her with restricted mobility and in a great deal of pain. After she had worked so hard, this assault meant that she would never be fit enough to return to frontline policing and dashed her dream of becoming a dog handler.

Kate continues to work as a police officer and has taken several office-based roles since the assault. She has shown so much compassion, integrity, and perseverance during her service. She was incredibly lucky to survive the car accident and it was down to her sheer courage that she was able to push forward and return to the sharp end of policing. For her then to be assaulted and lose it all again is heartbreaking. Today, she is tired all the time as she is unable to get any restful sleep due to pain and discomfort, which ultimately restricts much of her daily life. This in turn has caused her mental state to deteriorate.

When the Covid pandemic took hold Kate began to work from home which has slightly improved her mental and physical problems. However, this is not sustainable in the long term, and it is likely that she will need to return to the workplace. It is not known if she will be able to do that, and if she can't then the future of her career will be uncertain. Despite everything, there is still no holding Kate back. She and Ian are now happily married and share their house with their "hybrid dog" Missy whom they rescued from Romania.

The British police rightly are believed to be the best in the world, and Kate embodies everything that is exceptional about them. She is resilient, honest, kind, and unafraid to stand up for what is right. She deserves the utmost respect for her bravery in her continuing battle to live a good life despite life-changing injury.

PC FIONA BONE
(GREATER MANCHESTER POLICE)

At thirty-two years old, Fiona was probably the happiest that she had ever been. The previous Christmas she had moved into the home in Sale that her partner shared with her five-year-old daughter. The couple had met through mutual friends and were deeply in love. On the 29th of February 2012, her partner used the leap year tradition to ask Fiona to marry her. With the proposal accepted, they were excited to plan the wedding, with a date set for May 2021. Fiona (or Fi as she was usually known) was planning to adopt her partner's child when they were married, and described picking the little girl up from school as the best part of her day. It was clear to all that Fiona was going to be a fantastic co-parent, drawing on her passion for adventure, cycling, swimming, and camping.

Fiona had been an officer with Greater Manchester Police (GMP) for five years, and it was a job she excelled at. She was well respected by her colleagues in a tight-knit team, but it was her bubbly personality that made her special as it brought them together during difficult times. She was based at Hyde Police Station on the Tameside division which covered the eastern edges of the force's jurisdiction and its border with Derbyshire. Despite the semi-rural location there were several tough estates and towns which kept the officers extremely busy.

Shortly before seven on the morning of the 18th of September 2012, the oncoming day shift were starting to settle down, ready for their briefing. There were just six officers present, and they were in good spirits as they had been helping Fiona to design her wedding invitations. At the briefing the sergeant went through the intelligence and information that the team needed to know prior to commencing their shift. Initially Fiona had been tasked to work alone and her friend PC Nicola Hughes had been tasked to work with an officer whom I will refer to as "Mark" however, this was changed when Nicola asked Mark to swap with her so that she could work with Fiona. They were keen to chat about the wedding preparations if they had time between incidents. Now Fiona and Nicola were tasked to work on a divisional van, call sign Golf Mike Four One, with Nicola choosing to drive. They were soon given their first job: a simple prisoner transfer to the neighbouring division. Nicola was twenty-three and had been a police officer for three years. She was trim and looked younger than her years, with colleagues joking that she looked like a schoolgirl in a police uniform; nevertheless, she was no pushover and would wade into a pub fight with the best of them. Although she was feisty, her sergeant described her as a chatterbox who was vibrant and funny; someone who always had something to say.

At 10.36 that morning the police control room received a call to the emergency switchboard from a man who reported that someone had thrown a concrete slab through his back window. He gave his address as 30 Abbey Gardens, Hattersley. The caller claimed to be the resident; however, he was a wanted man who had taken over the house from the family who lived there at the time. He was a small-time drug dealer who had achieved nothing in his life. Desperate to be someone, he had escalated a dispute between two crime families to the point that he was now wanted for the murders of a father and his son. With that call, he set in motion a premeditated ambush: he didn't care who would respond; he was simply intent on attacking the police. If anyone was in any doubt as to his intention that day, his final chilling words to the call taker were "I will be waiting." Indeed, he was waiting and watching, armed with a Glock pistol loaded with an extended magazine, and a Yugoslavian hand grenade.

As Fiona and Nicola were now back on patrol and nearby, they were tasked to deal with the call. As Nicola drove into Abbey Gardens, the killer was cowering behind the curtains as he watched the police van drive down the long cul-de-sac to the bottom. He watched both officers get out and approach the front door. At this point he could still have given up and allowed himself to be taken into custody. He did not. Instead, he continued his cowardly attack with pistol in hand, he opened the door before the officers even knocked, and instantly began shooting, hitting each officer once in the chest. In this case they were saved by their body armour, and Nicola turned to run straight back towards the gate to get out of the garden. He continued to shoot at her until a bullet passed below the bottom of her body armour and severed her spinal cord. She fell, paralysed, but still alive. Fiona, who had moved sideways across the small garden, was now outside the front window of the house. Despite witnessing what had happened to Nicola, she heroically stood her ground and drew her Taser electronic stun gun. It is likely that she took a sideways stance to make herself a smaller target before raising her Taser in the attacker's direction. Although she fired at him, it missed. Terrifyingly the gunman turned on her and fired twenty-two bullets, most of which were absorbed by her body armour or missed her. However, as she turned a single bullet passed between the front and back panels of her body armour and entered her rising aorta. Fiona died almost immediately. Turning back to Nicola, the gunman leaned over her and fired three times at her head and face. Alive and unable to move, she must have been terrified.

He then ran towards a stolen BMW, pausing only to throw the grenade into the garden. It landed close to Nicola and the explosion inflicted further devastating injuries upon her body. Watching from the upstairs room of the house were a woman and child whom the gunman had held hostage overnight whilst he held a solitary going-away party for himself, during which he had got drunk and taken drugs. The killer then drove the BMW at speeds of up to one hundred miles an hour to the safety of Hyde Police Station where he planned to turn himself in.

By now the police switchboard was dealing with emergency calls that were coming in from the neighbours, and the radio dispatchers were desperately trying to contact Golf Mike Four One. The GPS in both officers' radios confirmed that they were on scene, and all the other officers on the radio channel were holding out to hear Fiona or Nicola respond, but the silence was palpable.

While this was happening, the murderer entered the police station and was standing at the front counter. In the back room an officer was desperately listening to his radio hoping for good news. Aware that someone had entered he glanced at the CCTV screen and instantly recognised the wanted man. Despite the serious news he was hearing over the radio, he stepped forward and vaulted the counter to arrest and handcuff him. In doing so he showed incredible bravery as he didn't know if the man was still armed or if he was being lured into another ambush.

At the divisional headquarters in Ashton-under-Lyne, Chief Superintendent Nick Adderley, the divisional commander, was chairing the morning meeting when a clearly shocked detective unceremoniously flung open the conference-room door and beckoned him outside without saying a word. Nick Adderley quickly established what was going on and immediately took control of the situation by contacting and speaking to the officers who had attended Abbey Gardens to back up Fiona and Nicola. Despite the unimaginable horror that faced them, they had done everything possible to stabilise their friend Nicola until an Ambulance could get through and take her to the hospital, where she too passed away.

Mark was one of the first officers to arrive at the scene and he and the others demonstrated extreme bravery as none of them could have known if the killer had set booby traps aimed at the first responders. A forensics tent was quickly erected to shield Fiona's body. As she had died where she'd fallen, her remains now formed part of the crime scene and would not be recovered until the next morning after the scene-of-crime officers had gathered their evidence. Paul Bone, Fiona's father, told me just how grateful and touched he had been to know that Nick Adderley had chosen to stay on duty, and, in an act of exceptional leadership and compassion, he remained at the scene to ensure that Fiona would not be left alone overnight.

Mark was deeply affected by what he had seen and felt responsible for the loss of his friends. Paul said, "I met Mark a couple of times; he was such a good man. I know that he blamed himself, but he should never have done; he had done nothing wrong." Mark went on to suffer from post-traumatic stress disorder and depression, and left the police in 2015. In the early hours of the 30th of August, the following year, he suffered a serious setback in his recovery. Despondent, he began to send messages to his friends and colleagues saying that he intended to kill himself. He was later found hanging in a small park in Stalybridge; in a tragic irony it was in the same place where he had once discovered a deceased person while walking his dog. When the police recovered his body and searched his pockets, they found that he had completed the official forms that police use to record a sudden death, along with the wristband used to identify the deceased. A police officer to the end, even in death Mark wanted to help his colleagues. He died just over two weeks before the fourth anniversary of the deaths of his friends.

Fiona was the second daughter of Paul and June Bone, who had been married for five years when she arrived. Her older sister Victoria was just a toddler when Fiona was born on New Year's Eve 1979. Paul was an aircraft engineer in the Royal Air Force (RAF), stationed at Swanton Morley at the time. Fiona was a little over one year old when he was restationed to RAF Lossiemouth in Scotland. Here she would grow up and complete her primary education. She loved her time in Scotland and, although English, she always considered herself a proud Scot. Paul remembers a happy little girl who made friends easily. She was also very loyal and would stay in touch with her friends long after she had moved on. In fact, Paul says that, at the time of her death, "she had friends all over the place; it was hard to keep up with them all." When she was twelve, Paul retired from the RAF and the family moved to Castle Donington in Leicestershire.

Paul then became a civilian instructor with the Air Training Corps and Fiona joined as a cadet. She had some notion of becoming a pilot, and enjoyed the flying experience in a Bulldog training plane. It was a two-seater, and, unlike the old Chipmunks, she was able to sit next to the pilot instead of behind them. Soon she took a flight with a colleague of Paul's who had a private pilot's licence. In the air, Fiona was able to take the controls. She then asked the pilot if she could take some photos. He was amazed when she then dug out her camera and began taking pictures whilst maintaining a perfectly steady course. However, the urge to become a pilot soon faded as, apart from the take-off and the landing, she found the actual flying a bit boring and she did not want to be a bus driver in the sky.

Fiona was seventeen when the family moved to the Isle of Man, where she joined the sixth form at Castle Rushen High School so that she could complete her A Levels in English, general studies, and computer studies. Her personality shone and she was soon welcomed into a group of friends. One of them, Juan Watterson, now the Speaker of the House in the Isle of Man Parliament, remembers, "She came to us late in our school lives, but it wasn't long before it felt like she had been with us since she was four. She was bubbly and great fun; she could make us do anything. I remember a time when we all squeezed ourselves into a phone box because she wanted to know how many people it would hold." Mr Fife, Fiona's former tutor at Castle Rushen, remembered her as having a "great sense of responsibility, and she was totally reliable." These qualities no doubt supported her in becoming such a good officer.

Fiona had a great deal of compassion, and she was extremely caring and kind, and it was no surprise that she chose to work with older people when it came to the service aspect of her Duke of Edinburgh Gold Award. As for her community spirit, she also enrolled with the St John's ambulance and trained with the service until July 1999 when she started studying for a degree in audiovisual media and film studies at the University of Central Lancashire.

At the end of her first term, she returned to the Isle of Man for Christmas. Juan recalls New Year's Eve that year, as it was also Fiona's twentieth birthday. The group of friends had gone on a long walk out to Cregneash, a small rural museum located on Mull Hill to the south-west of the island. "It was the perfect place to huddle up together and watch the sun go down for the last time before moving into a new millennium," he said. "Those were the best of times. We were all looking to the future. At the time Fiona had not shown any interest in joining the police; she was a counsellor, a listener, and always gave the best advice. In hindsight I think that is what made her such a great police officer. The group separated for a while so that we could each spend some time with our families before meeting up again in the pub opposite Fiona's house for a lock-in. Stumbling from the pub, a little worse for wear, in the early hours, Fiona suggested we go back to her house. We didn't want to go crashing through the front door making a load of noise, which would wake everybody up, so Fiona led us around the back, where we climbed straight into the house through the kitchen window for mugs of hot tea and toast."

After completing her degree in 2002, Fiona was back on the island and started playing rugby for the Vagabonds. She also took a course in film production and became involved in making the movie *Blackball*, which starred Vince Vaughn and Imelda Staunton. Her father said that she did not work on the main set with the actors; instead, she "mostly stood around in the pouring rain, stopping cars". This too was first-class training for her future in the police. With the course funding coming to an end, she started looking around for her next adventure. Paul said, "She wanted to move somewhere more exciting, where the pace of life was quicker." She narrowed down her choice to either Manchester or Leeds. In the end she opted for Manchester and moved over, getting a job with an insurance company in the city centre. Insurance work soon proved to be routine, if not a little boring and she was looking for a new challenge.

In a decision that surprised most, she applied to join GMP as a special constable. A special constable is a fully warranted police officer; however, they are unpaid volunteers who give up their free time to support full-time officers. The time and commitment that they put into policing makes them a great asset. Fiona took to police work like a duck to water and in 2007 or 2008 after nearly two years as a special constable, made the leap and joined up full time. Her excellent work was soon recognised, and in 2009 she was awarded a chief superintendent's commendation for her "outstanding contribution in an investigation into a series of burglaries and robberies which secured convictions." Paul said, "Fiona was never one to flaunt her successes, and we didn't even know about the commendation until it was mentioned at her funeral." He smiled when he remembered one of the few stories that Fiona had told him about her job: "Apparently there were loads of them fighting with a violent drug dealer, anyway, Fiona decided to use her pepper spray and, in the end, she sprayed all her colleagues. I think that was the first and last time that she ever tried to use it."

Fiona's funeral took place on the 4th of October 2012 at Manchester Cathedral, just a day after her working partner Nicola had been laid to rest. As they had the day before, hundreds of mourners lined Deansgate and the entrance to the cathedral. As well as the many locals there were police officers who felt compelled to attend, some from all over the country. Only a few knew Fiona personally, but all needed to pay their respects and honour her bravery. The funeral cortège was escorted to the cathedral by six police horses, their riders wearing full ceremonial uniform, as the crowd threw roses onto the bonnet of the hearse. Paul recalled, "It was overwhelming to see so many people lining the streets." Spontaneous applause broke out as the cortège turned into the small courtyard in front of the cathedral. A police guard of honour was positioned outside the cathedral's imposing front door. Fiona's coffin was draped in a black flag which sported a large, embroidered GMP badge on the top. Alongside it was her police hat and gloves and her Queen's Diamond Jubilee Medal. As the pall-bearers (one of whom was Mark) shouldered her coffin, a lone piper struck up a haunting lament and they led the funeral party into the cathedral. Behind them, a uniformed officer carried a large colour photo of Fiona smiling with pleasure.

The service was then broadcast to the crowds by way of loudspeakers. Mourners clutching curled copies of the order of service stood in the cold, listening intently as Fiona's sergeant addressed them: "Fiona was wonderful. She was wonderful at keeping colleagues' spirits high with her bubbly nature. She was wonderful about caring for others. Fiona represented the best that humanity has to offer the world, but that makes her loss even greater." Sir Peter Fahy the chief constable described Fiona as a "calm, gentle woman". He added, "When she first joined the shift, she was quite quiet and reserved. However, she came out of her shell and had a great sense of humour and always enjoyed a good laugh. She was so happy with her partner, and they were in the middle of planning their wedding. Indeed, her partner had only spoken to her that morning about the wedding invites." (The same invites that her friends had been helping her with before the fateful shift.) He continued, "Her fellow officers said they loved being partnered with her because she was always calm, collected and professional, and could calm situations with her gentle way."

After an hour, the funeral came to an end. The piper played another lament as Fiona's coffin was respectfully carried outside and returned to the hearse, which would take her to her final resting place, and a private burial in her beloved Scotland.

On the 9th of May 2013, Paul was invited to lay a memorial stone in honour of Fiona on a £7.8 million building project in Sale, the town where she had lived with her partner. The building would flourish into a seventy-one-apartment complex where vulnerable adults and older people could be assisted to live independently. The complex – which was equipped with landscaped gardens, a restaurant, and sensory rooms would come to be named Fiona Gardens in her memory. It was officially opened on the 1st of October 2014. The memorial stone features prominently, just to the left of the main entrance. In an interview Fiona's sister Vicky said, "Fiona was most passionate about working with the elderly and young people; it was the human side of policing that she really enjoyed. It was the vulnerable that Fiona was there to protect, and to have this named after her is an honour and a privilege. She would have absolutely loved it."

The Police Memorial Trust was established by film director Michael Winner following the murder of PC Yvonne Fletcher, who was shot by an unknown person firing from inside the Iranian Embassy in London on the 17th of April 1984. The trust lays memorial stones in honour of fallen officers, at or near the site where they were killed. However, after discussion with the people of Hattersley, Fiona and Nicola's stone was not erected in Abbey Gardens but a short distance away at the "Hub" community centre. It was unveiled on the 14th of July 2016 by David Cameron, who until the day before had been the British Prime Minister. His successor was Theresa May, the previous Home Secretary who was apparently too busy forming her new cabinet to attend. In the wake of Fiona's death, her family would meet hundreds of people. However, Theresa May was the only one that Paul refused to meet: "Fiona had hated the way that she was destroying the police with her devastating budget cuts. Officers were now overworked and usually patrolled alone, putting them under more stress and putting them in increasingly dangerous situations." A second stone was laid at Hyde Police Station, from which Fiona and Nicola had worked. Remembering the day, Paul said, "Nick Adderley was there, but he stayed right in the background like he didn't want to be noticed and draw any attention away from the service. It was a shame as I would have liked to have talked to him some more, but I appreciated what he was doing."

In the many hours that I spent talking to Paul via Zoom, I often noticed the triangular stars and stripes flag which was framed and hung on the wall behind him. Intrigued, I asked him about it. He explained that he was involved with a charity named Care of Police Survivors (COPS), a peer support organisation which offers support to those who have lost a member of the family who was a police officer. Paul explained that a representative of COPS usually travels over to Washington for the National Police Memorial Day on the 15th of May. Hundreds of flags were flown over the US capital, two of which were ceremonially folded and brought back to the UK, where they were presented to the families of Fiona and Nicola. That same year, the Police Federation awarded Fiona and Nicola the Women in Policing Award. This was particularly poignant as that year's conference celebrated the fact that women had been serving in the police for one hundred years. The chair of the federation said, "Fiona and Nicola's sacrifice will be forever etched in our hearts."

VIOLENCE AGAINST
THE POLICE

In the UK, violence against the police continues to rise to unprecedented levels. In 2021 there were 36,369 assaults on police officers in England and Wales; a 20% increase from the previous year, which itself saw a further 20% increase from 2019's figures. To put that into context, it equates to 720 assaults a week, 101 each day, or four officers assaulted every single hour.

Any assault on the police is extremely serious; however, the nature of the violence they now face is almost unprecedented. In May 2019, officers in Essex were trying to make an arrest on a housing estate when a resident came out and threw a watering can full of petrol over them. The hostile crowd who had gathered chanted that the officers should be set alight. Two officers were later hospitalised due to ingestion of the fuel. It could be argued that they were lucky that they were not set alight, as in November 2020 an officer in Cornwall was indeed set on fire whilst dealing with a man, and suffered burns to his hands and legs.

Assaults with knives and other bladed weapons are an ever-increasing threat. In June 2021 an officer intervened after witnessing a drug deal. Two men were able to pin him down while a third slashed his throat. The officer was lucky to survive the four-inch wound. Increasingly, officers work alone and, as most UK officers are still unarmed, they only have an extendable baton and a can of CS or PAVA spray with which to defend themselves.

Although some front-line officers are now also issued with Tasers, they are far from the norm, which is unfortunate as in many circumstances possessing one is an incredible defensive tool as proved to be the case in August 2019. Police stopped a van in London and the driver, a violent criminal, attacked an officer with a machete that had a blade two feet long. The officer received dreadful wounds to his arm and head, and several of his fingers were broken and three of his tendons severed. If the officer had not been able to incapacitate the attacker his life would have been at significant risk.

Nick Adderley, who had already shown incredible compassion and leadership when he spent the night looking after the body of PC Fiona Bone, became the chief constable of Northamptonshire Police on the 6th of August 2018. Within weeks of the incident in London he became the first chief constable in the country to announce that he would issue a Taser to every front-line officer in the force who wanted to carry one. Although, the chief constable of Durham Constabulary quickly followed suit. However, police officers up and down the country are still patrolling alone and without the proper tools to protect themselves. This is scandalous and needs to be addressed as a matter of urgency.

A week after the London attack, an officer in Berkshire was killed when he was dragged by a vehicle escaping a burglary. The officer was dragged for a mile (1.6 kilometres) before his body became detached from the vehicle. In fact, vehicles are regularly used to assault officers: in another case on the 5th of October 2015 an officer was killed in Liverpool while standing on a central reservation waiting to throw out a stinger to deflate the tyres of a vehicle being chased by his colleagues. The driver appeared to deliberately mount the pavement to hit the officer.

Unfortunately, our police officers are not even safe from assault when off duty. On the 19th of December 2014, PC Neil Doyle, who had been married for just six months, was out for a Christmas drink with colleagues in Liverpool city centre. Along with PCs Robert Marshall and Michael Steventon, he was approached by two thugs, one of whom asked PC Doyle, "Are you having a good evening, Officer?" The officers attempted to walk away, but they were followed and subjected to a vicious and unprovoked attack. PC Doyle was punched in the head twice before he staggered across the road and collapsed in a gutter, where he lay dying. PC Marshall was kicked and punched, the victim of a wounding with intent, while PC Steventon suffered a fractured cheekbone. In the victim's personal statement, it was stated that PC Doyle's widow said, "Seeing him lying in a gutter like a dying cat, not one person going over to help, I will never get the image out of my head. My last words to him were: "I love you, stay safe and ring me when you want me to come and pick you up. I'm still waiting for that call."

Moreover, officers are not even safe in their own homes. In another horrendous example, an off-duty officer in Essex was at home on the 24th of April 2019 when he answered the door and was subjected to a frenzied knife attack in front of his wife and children. He was stabbed eleven times before he managed to overpower and restrain the attacker.

What I have addressed above is not the exception to the norm; it *is* the norm of policing in Britain in the twenty-first century. Far too many officers are being killed or seriously injured where their lives are changed forever as they must come to terms with what has happened to them. The injuries sustained have an impact not only on the officers themselves and their families, but also on their colleagues who witness or subsequently investigate the incident.

SERGEANT "DAVID"
(GREATER MANCHESTER POLICE)

David first dipped his toe into undercover work when he and a female colleague walked into a pub looking to buy drugs. Leaning against the bar, he struck up a conversation with the target. "Yeah, we're new around here," he said, "but I'm told that this is the place to come if you're looking for a good time." After a little bit of verbal sparring, the deal was done. David added, "We would drink up before going back to the safe location, where we would write up our notes and identify the key players from the surveillance footage. We would drop into the pub over the next couple of weekends, making further drug buys and gathering further evidence.

"The last time we went there to buy, we knew that the place was going to be raided. We were sitting at a table when the police flooded into the pub. A plain-clothes officer had photographs of all the arrest subjects, and to keep our cover in place our photographs were included. None of the officers involved knew we were undercover; as far as they were concerned, we were just drug users.

"The next thing I knew was that a couple of officers from the tactical aid unit grabbed me and after cuffing me, they dragged me outside before throwing me across the bonnet of the police van.

It's essential to stay in character the whole time, so I constantly shouted and resisted them. When the officers finally had me in their van, they explained what was going to happen to me. It was odd because I knew exactly what was going on. When we got to the police station, and while they were waiting to take me into custody, an officer from the undercover unit came and took me from the arresting officers and we effectively walked off into the sunset. My colleague wasn't as lucky as she had already been booked into custody and was sitting in a cell after giving her name as Minnie Mouse. Once she was out, we went back to the safe location, did our statements, and that was it. I had done my first spell undercover."

The following afternoon, David was back in the locker room at Stockport Police Station, getting kitted up for a late shift. It is a misconception that undercover officers work undercover permanently. Instead, each has their own job, and they are deployed as and when they are required. David had become involved in undercover work after a sergeant who had been a surveillance officer was promoted to his team. Although David had only just completed his probation, the sergeant spotted his potential, so, David applied and was sent on a gruelling week-long course in which he was taught how to build a legend (an identity that he would use while undercover) and how to deal with threats he might face when he got out onto the streets and tried to buy drugs. A keen boxer since the age of eleven, David had a very slim physique which he used to his advantage when building his legend: "I took on the persona of a heroin user. I kept a bag of dirty clothes that I would wear when I was on a job, and they stunk after being tied up in a plastic bag for months on end. I looked like a complete bag of shit and exactly like the type of person I would've stopped and searched if I had seen them while on patrol."

However, his initial undercover deployments weren't on the housing estates and the backstreets of Manchester, instead he was deployed to the city's raves and nightclubs that were becoming world famous. "We would get into the clubs and just keep our eyes peeled for dealers. A good tactic was to go to the toilets, and if I saw anybody dealing, I would say something like, 'can I get in on that?' At the time we were buying mostly ecstasy and cocaine." It took an immense amount of courage to do what he was doing, as organised crime groups were fighting a vicious war for control of the doors in the city centre. To control the doors with your own bouncers was to control who was able to sell drugs inside the venue. Any dealer caught selling drugs inside was likely to take a serious beating and have their drugs stolen and sold on. It is only down to the hard work of David and his colleagues that the police were eventually able to gather evidence and plan operations that would bring some degree of order to the city. David smiled when he said, "We were successful everywhere except the "Gay Village" where we were blown out before we could even get into the pubs and clubs."

Ever the high achiever, he continued to box while in the police, and was regularly selected to represent the British Police both at home and internationally, where he boxed against officers from Italy, the Bahamas and the USA. After four and a half years at Stockport he moved to the tactical aid unit (TAU), a team of highly motivated officers who work throughout the force. The unit are experts, trained in dealing with large-scale disorder, crowd control, and counterterrorism. At that time the TAU was tasked to operate in specific areas across the force, only coming together for major incidents. David's team was responsible for the city centre and South Manchester including Moss Side, then dubbed 'Gunchester' by the national media due to its high levels of gun and gang crime. The TAU took on these violent drug gangs directly by finding and seizing their drugs and weapons, and developing intelligence which would allow them to use various proactive strategies as well as a focus on disrupting street dealing.

As David was on the TAU, he was one of a half a dozen officers working on a van. Therefore, he could be spared more easily, and it was now possible for him to take on long-term undercover operations. Although his colleagues would never know what he was doing. As such keeping this side of his career secret could be problematic. Soon after joining the TAU, he spent a week on a course with one of the officers who had arrested him on his first deployment. Throughout the week the officer insisted that he recognised David and focused all his attention on figuring out how they knew each other, whilst he was forced to insist that they had never met. He would soon go undercover in the towns to the east and west of Manchester, where he was unlikely to be known as a police officer. "It started off with me going out to a phone box and cold-calling suspected drug dealers so that I could arrange to buy heroin or crack from them. Most of the time they would agree to sell, and I would wait near the phone box for them to come and make the deal. I always had to be sure that I stayed in character as there was always a chance that the dealer might send someone out to watch me if they were suspicious. When they sold me the drugs, I would take a phone number so that I could buy from them again." As David was starting to be recognised, he began to befriend users and take their phone numbers.

In all, David was undercover for close to a year and bought drugs from forty to fifty different dealers. In some cases, the dealers wanted to sell drugs in larger quantities. As a Level 2 officer David had a maximum budget of £60; therefore, he would introduce the dealer to Level 1 officers who were better equipped to deal with that type of operation. He recalled how there was an inherent risk in buying drugs: "I had arranged to buy from a new dealer who turned up in a car with another guy in the front passenger seat. The passenger then pulled a knife and insisted that I get in the car and take the drugs with them. For obvious reasons I couldn't do that, so I chucked him ten quid, saying that I had already been ripped off. Luckily, he just threw me the gear before they drove away."

Towards the end of the 1990s, organised football violence was becoming a serious national issue. This was just the type of environment that would bring the TAU together. On the 6th of February 1999 Millwall supporters came north for a return match against Manchester City. The year before there had been serious disorder in London, and a repeat was expected. However, what the police hadn't anticipated was that a fight had been arranged for before the match. Stockport had been picked as the location as it was the last stop on the train from London before it reached Manchester.

David said, "We were the first TAU van to get there. It was complete carnage as there were running battles involving more than five hundred people. There were six or seven of us running with shields, trying to keep them apart. It wasn't long before further TAU vans arrived, and we were slowly able to get them under control. As soon as there were enough of us to manage the situation, we corralled them before pushing them back to the train station and onto the train to Manchester. As soon as they were on the train we ran back to our vehicles and raced the train to Piccadilly in a convoy of vans on blues and twos so that we could meet them off the train and escort them to the Manchester City stadium which was about three miles away.

"Once we had got all the supporters into the ground, we went to get a brew, but we didn't get chance as we were called into the stadium because it had kicked off. The supporters were kept apart by police officers who were trying to hold a small, segregated area between them. The supporters were tearing up seats and throwing them at each other, and the officers in the middle were getting battered. It was absolute war in the stadium, and I can honestly say that it was the most intense and sustained violence I've ever faced as a police officer."

Coincidently, BBC journalist Donal MacIntyre was making the *Panorama* programme *'Headhunters'*, a documentary about his time undercover with the hooligans following Chelsea Football Club. In the film, which aired in 2000, he described the incident as "the season's biggest outbreak of violence". Following the match there were several violent clashes in nearby Rusholme; however, the TAU managed to contain the supporters and walk them back to Manchester, where they were put on trains back to London.

While on the TAU he passed his promotion assessments and later in the year he was promoted to the rank of acting sergeant in South Manchester. In this role he gained a reputation for being strict but fair and earned a great deal of respect, as he always led from the front and never asked anyone to do anything that he hadn't done himself. When he was substantively promoted in 2002, he was transferred to the Tameside division. He had not wanted to work on that division as he also lived on the division, but his protest fell on deaf ears. When he joined his new team, he supervised Fiona Bone and Nicola Hughes' future colleague Mark. David remembers him as being "a quiet man and a good, solid bobby whose tragic suicide was a massive loss to his colleagues and the communities that he had served".

David had only been working on the division a little over a year when he dealt with an incident that would change his life forever. "My team were on nights on the 3rd of September 2003, and during the shift I had been out on foot patrol. I had done that as I had a probationary officer on the team who was reluctant to do it themselves. My intention was to set an example before making it clear that the officer and others were required to follow my orders and carry out these patrols. The shift went off without incident and I went off duty just after seven on the morning of the 4th of September.

"As a shift worker it's always been my habit to either run five miles after work or, like I did that morning, go and swim a mile. If I didn't do the exercise I would struggle to get to sleep. I was home and eating breakfast in bed at around nine when I heard a noise outside. I went downstairs, and when I looked out of the window, I saw a man in my neighbour's garden. I immediately recognised him as a burglar, although I couldn't recall his name. I went into my garden and called 999, requesting back up and reporting that there was *"a thieves on"* at the address.

"I was concerned about my neighbour as she was an old lady who lived alone. Therefore, I didn't wait for officers to arrive before I checked out what was going on. I climbed over the fence and saw that the window was smashed, and the suspect had gained entry. I called 999 again and now requested *"emergency assistance"* before entering the house, which was a traditional two-up, two-down. The stairs were in the middle of the two bottom rooms. Looking up the stairs, I saw the male come out of the front bedroom and onto the landing, I challenged him, and I identified myself as a police officer.' The burglar replied, 'Well, you ain't fuckin stoppin' me' and I noticed that he had two screwdrivers sticking out of his pocket. The burglar came rushing down the stairs. I immediately tried to get a grip of him. During the struggle we ended up on the floor with him above me. I had my lower back arched as I was trying to pull his top over his head, as I had been thinking about securing DNA that would convict him. My initial police training kicked in and I used the grappling skills that I had been taught. As I was doing this, I didn't know that he had got hold of a screwdriver and was trying to stab my exposed back. As I had his top over his head, the guy stood up, and as he was much bigger than me, he pulled me up too. As he did so I was conscious that I needed to put some distance between us for my safety, so I hit him in the face twice, as hard as I could, with my dominant right hand. He reeled back, and as I was still holding his top; it came off him completely. I now noticed that he had a screwdriver in his right hand, and he lunged at me, saying, 'I'm gonna fuckin' kill yer now! The screwdriver was aimed at my chest. I thought, *oh shit, I'd better get out of here.* Fortunately, I was very close to the back door and managed to get outside as he lunged at me, I managed to slam the door on the screwdriver. I believe this probably saved my life."

David was now outside with the burglar inside. Despite being alone, he was darting between the front and back of the house to prevent the burglar's escape. While he was at the front the first patrol arrived at the scene. One of the officers saw that the back of David's T-shirt was drenched with blood. David said, "With the adrenalin pumping I had assumed that it was just sweat. Anyway, there was no time to deal with it if we were going to catch the burglar. I told the officers to follow me into the house round the back. Unfortunately, he had managed to escape in the meantime."

When the officers checked his injuries, they discovered several deep slash wounds, which had been caused when the burglar had attempted to stab him as he lay on his back during their tussle. It was the first time that he realised just how close he had been to losing his life or his ability to walk. He was taken to hospital, where his wounds were stitched. It was also discovered that he had torn ligaments in his badly swollen hand, sustained when he had punched the burglar.

Later that day, the suspect was traced and arrested on suspicion of attempted murder and burglary. On the arrest the burglar said, "I didn't stab him," even though both screwdrivers were recovered from his car. Later David had no hesitation in formally identifying him. David had intended to go back to work the same night, and only reported sick when he was ordered to do so. He was told to keep his police radio at home with him so that he could call for assistance in the event of further problems. Three weeks later he heard suspicious noises outside, but when he tried to put the battery into his radio, he was unable to do so as his hands were shaking so much. He informed his supervisors and was sent for an assessment, following which he was diagnosed with PTSD and began to see a psychologist.

He eventually returned to work in December. In retrospect, he recognises that this was too soon, and he was probably not ready. However, that is often the case with hard-working and dedicated officers who put other's needs before their own. Now that he was back, he looked at the status of his investigation, only to learn that the detective who had been investigating the case had let him down massively. First, the officer had accepted a lesser charge of grievous bodily harm instead of attempted murder. They had also updated the crime report, stating that he had been informed of the new charge and was happy with it. In fact, this was the first time that he had learned of it. The detective had also failed to submit the screwdrivers for DNA testing, which would have proved that the blood on them belonged to David. It was now too late to gather that evidence as the DNA had diminished. Finally, David realised that the detective had also not taken a statement from the doctor who had stitched his wounds, which would have confirmed that they were consistent with a screwdriver attack.

Therefore, he had to send his own officers out to get the statement just three weeks before the start of the trial. That statement proved crucial as when the case came to court it forced the burglar to change his plea and admit his guilt. Before being taken down to the cells, he shouted at David, "I'm gonna come for yer."

On his second night back at work, David stopped and searched a suspicious man and found that he was carrying a screwdriver. This triggered his PTSD and hypervigilance, and consequently he made a couple of minor errors when dealing with the situation. The following day he was dragged in front of a senior officer, who demanded that he account for himself. That officer would have known about the stabbing, which had happened less than three months before; despite that, he never considered that David might need further support. Even though working on the Tameside division remained a significant trigger for David's PTSD, he continued to work there for a further nine months, although he regularly requested a transfer. In the end, a senior officer who was a close friend and understood his situation moved him back to South Manchester and tasked him with hand-picking officers to address the growing threat posed by gang and gun crime in Wythenshawe, one of the largest public housing estates in Europe. However, David was not intimidated by the scale of the problem, and deployed his team to carry out proactive patrols targeting the gang members who were at the heart of the problem. The team achieved many successes, from arresting and convicting key players to seizing weapons. In one operation they targeted pubs on the estate after receiving intelligence that there was a gun in the area. As they entered a pub, a man was seen to dump a loaded handgun behind the bar. The police met with hostile resistance from the customers, but quickly gained control of the situation. The handgun was seized along with a quantity of drugs. The police would score a further success when they applied to have the premises' licence removed and the pub was permanently shut.

In March 2005, with crime on the estate declining, David finally landed his dream job and was appointed as the officer safety training (OST) sergeant, also known as the force physical training instructor (PTI). At that time, the police forces across England and Wales were starting a huge recruitment drive, resulting in Greater Manchester Police gaining more than a thousand extra officers. Although this was excellent news in the war against crime, it had an adverse effect on the amount of training that existing officers received. OST is a package of training wherein an officer is taught the legislation around the use of force and self-defence, as well as how to use their personal protective equipment (PPE), baton, handcuffs and CS spray, and physical restraint techniques. However, as with all things, this training needs to be regularly refreshed. National guidelines stated that police officers needed two days of refreshment every year; however, at the time officers in

Greater Manchester received one day or six hours. Not long after he was appointed to the post, that training was reduced further to one day every eighteen months. Refresher training is essential as it allows the training staff to assess whether officers are using their equipment safely and correctly, and update them with any new techniques. This is essential both to ensure that officers have the knowledge and training to defend themselves against violence, and to prevent suspects from being injured during arrest.

From the outset, David raised his concerns about the situation. "No matter how often I raised the situation, I was ignored. They just acted as if 'the mad sergeant is moaning again'. It was clear that my PTSD was used as a reason to disregard what I was saying and to undermine my concerns." He became suspicious that his supervision was not passing his concerns on to the force's senior leadership team. The problem got so bad that 2,500 officers were at risk of losing their authorisation to carry their PPE. Believing that he had no other option, David emailed the chief superintendent on every division, listing the officers who should no longer be deployed on the streets. His email caused such a stir that he was called to appear before the assistant chief constable (ACC). At that meeting the ACC had intended to discipline him. That was until David laid out all the facts to support his action, it turned out he had been correct as the senior leadership team had not been made aware of the issue.

When the police regional training centres were closed in 2006, new recruits started to be trained within their own force. To ensure that they got the best possible start David developed a two-week OST package for them. As a result, the officers would be properly prepared to protect themselves and the public whilst also reducing the risk of injury to everyone involved. David fought for four years for this package to be rolled out to special constables as they only received three days' training on joining. Finally in 2010 they began to be trained at the same level as regular officers. As he said, "They might be volunteers, but they are police officers, and they deserve the same standard of training as anyone else."

One Friday afternoon in late 2007 or early 2008, David was at work when he received a phone call informing him that the burglar who had stabbed him had escaped from an open prison. As there was a significant chance that he would carry out his threats, it was essential that David was protected. However, it was left to him to find somebody with the authority to approve the fitting of a personal attack alarm at his home. It was fortunate that he was able to contact the friend who had assisted him in the past, as his own supervisors and senior command team were off duty for the weekend. The fact is that somebody should have immediately taken proactive steps to safeguard him and not leave it to him to sort out.

It was also around this time that David discovered that the police had also been aware of threats which had been made against him by the organised crime group that he had tackled in Oldham as an undercover officer. It transpired that when he was going to be posted as a substantive sergeant he was supposed to be posted to Oldham; however, although the threats had been serious enough for that plan to be changed, nobody had bothered to tell him about them. It is also a terrible indictment on the criminal justice system that a violent burglar can walk away from an open prison within two years of being sentenced. It is no wonder that violent crime is now out of control.

Although he had been let down massively, David like so many other officers is extremely resilient and he continued to work hard to improve the training that his colleagues would receive. When Tasers were rolled out to response officers, he developed a four-day course wherein officers received ten hours of training each day. "Those officers got the best OST training of all because we were able to revisit and reinforce so much of what they had already been taught." Soon the Metropolitan Police visited GMP to review the Taser package that David had developed. Impressed, they used it as a template when they rolled out Tasers to operational police officers in the capital. One of his students was PC Fiona Bone, David said, "She was incredibly brave, she had the presence of mind to put her training into practice, and did everything that she could do to protect herself, her colleague and the local residents."

As David was a trainer of trainers to the OST instructors, he was responsible for ensuring that they were up to delivering the courses correctly. Unfortunately, one instructor's performance was not acceptable. David worked hard to help him improve; however, it didn't work. David then learned that the man had been complaining about him and attempting to undermine his ability as a trainer on the grounds of his PTSD. In the end things got so bad that he spoke to a lawyer and took GMP to an employment tribunal for disability discrimination. The tribunal was never heard as the force decided to pay him damages. However, still nothing changed as he continued to be treated as the "mad sergeant". At some point in 2010 the force decided to reduce the number of sergeants in the OST unit from five to three.

Of the five sergeants in the office, he and two others were substantive in rank and two were on temporary promotion. David had the most qualifications in training OST and Taser as well as public order. A further factor that should have ensured that he stayed in post was that his PTSD had worsened, and he was no longer able to have working contact with the public. There was also the fact that he was the elected Police Federation representative supporting officers in the training department among others. In the circumstances it would be reasonable to assume that his position was safe. However, while on holiday he took a phone call informing him that the decision had been made that he would be redeployed. He had twenty-eight days to appeal the decision, and so submitted an appeal and had to deliver a thirty-minute presentation on why he should remain in post. Fortunately, he was successful.

Following the riots in the summer of 2011, Her Majesty's Inspectorate of Constabulary (HMIC) visited the force to review the training that officers received for OST and public order. Although David should have been the sergeant who was interviewed by the inspectors, he was prevented from doing so and another sergeant was nominated. At about the same time that the HMIC produced their report (which recommended that the force should reintroduce two days of training), David completed his diploma in management and leadership. During his studies he had researched how much time was lost because of officers being on sick leave due to a preventable assault, and the financial costs of investigating complaints relating to errors in the use of force, as well as compensation paid out to complainants, all of which would be preventable if officers were trained regularly. In fact, his findings demonstrated that reintroducing two days of training would save the force £1.5 million each year through the reduction in sickness and complaints, not to mention keeping officers safer while protecting the public and provided a compelling business case to support his assertions. David fought for seven years to achieve this. However, it would only be reintroduced six months after he retired.

The fight had been extremely hard, and had seriously impacted on his PTSD, making it impossible for him to recover while he remained in the police, and particularly the environment in which he was working. Therefore, in September 2012 he was retired from the force on grounds of ill health. He had served with distinction for just over twenty years, and been awarded numerous commendations from senior officers, judges and the FBI for leadership, bravery, professionalism and effective investigations. His service has gone a long way towards making Greater Manchester a safer place. However, none of that protected him from being subjected to discrimination because of his PTSD; something directly attributed to his heroic attempt to protect his elderly neighbour from being burgled. Today he still lives with the effects of his illness.

David's only solace throughout the years of torment was his beloved boxing; an activity in which he taught youngsters discipline, respect, and self-defence, and ultimately some became champions while he was the head coach of clubs in Tameside and Oldham. He is now a qualified international referee and a judge, representing England and Great Britain.

ILL-HEALTH
RETIREMENT

When an officer is injured on duty there are several potential pensions available to them. The Police Pension Authority (PPA) must first decide whether to retire the officer on grounds of ill health. They do this by referring them to an independent doctor known as a selected medical practitioner (SMP). The SMP must establish that the officer has a permanent disability, and that they are no longer capable of performing the ordinary duties of a police officer. If the PPA decide to retire the officer, the SMP will then consider whether the injury is an injury on duty (IOD) and, if so, the effect of that injury on the officer's earning capacity in regular employment. The degree of disablement is classified into four bands, and the greater the effect on earning capacity, the higher the band and the pension award. It is important to note that as the IOD award is paid by the officer's former force (and not the Home Office, as used to be the case), it is likely that the force will be motivated to save money. An officer retiring at thirty years of age is going to cost the force more money throughout the life of the pension compared to an officer retiring at fifty, particularly whose IOD is of a higher banding.

Forces have the right under the Police (Injury Benefit) Regulations 2006 to review the level of pension at suitable intervals, but it was due to Avon and Somerset Police unlawfully targeting a group of the youngest pensioners on the highest bands that the Injury on Duty Pensioners Association (IODPA) was formed back in 2014. These former officers began to support each other through a traumatic and adversarial process in which they were treated without empathy or compassion. The intention of these reviews was simply to save money by moving the officers onto a lower banding. Little did this small group know then that their work would grow into a national charity which now supports and assists injured police officers all over the UK with the legalities of the ill-health retirement (IHR) process, and the initial "award" and subsequent reviews of their IOD pensions.

IODPA's primary function is to empower officers and pensioners with a full understanding of the law and regulations that govern the IHR and IOD process, and to ensure that forces follow the letter of these rules. All too often, they see forces and their HR departments riding roughshod over people who are extremely vulnerable and who trust their force to do the right thing by them. Sadly, just a handful of forces do so and look after their injured colleagues correctly, mindful of the mental anguish the process causes even to those whose injuries are physical. The situation is so widespread that IODPA have now helped hundreds if not thousands of officers, and have members from every police force in the UK. The charity's trustees are not legally qualified and therefore do not give legal advice; however, where a legal issue is identified, officers are referred to legal professionals who ensure that they are treated correctly and within the regulations. Indeed, IODPA have held several forces to account when they have acted unlawfully.

It is a sad fact that police forces have extensive policies and procedures in place to protect criminals and ensure that they are treated with compassion and respect, and yet the same cannot be said when officers are treated poorly simply because they have been injured in the course of their duty. In recruit training they are told that they are now members of the police family and will be looked after. However, far too often they are abandoned and left to deal with their injuries and the IHR process alone. They have given so much to the force and the public that the realisation that it meant nothing to their superiors causes a further moral injury. They are deeply hurt by the betrayal. Their confidence is shattered, and the pride they once took in their service is replaced by embarrassment and a deep sense of rejection. This is tragic, and IODPA are working extremely hard to restore officers' self-belief and pride.

PC RICHARD HUBER
(SOUTH YORKSHIRE POLICE)

Born in Australia, Richard (or Rich as he is known to his friends) grew up with a passion for adventure, the great outdoors and sport, excelling at open-water swimming and rugby. Although good at sport he struggled a little at school, almost certainly due to undiagnosed attention deficit hyperactivity disorder (ADHD). Indeed, when asked to describe himself at that time, he said, "I was easily distracted and acted as the class clown."

His parents were Germans who had emigrated to Australia as a young couple. Although Rich recalls a strict "Germanic" upbringing he is grateful for the values that came with it, like integrity, hard work and personal responsibility. He also has great empathy and a genuine desire to protect and help people. With such a strong moral compass it should come as no surprise that he wanted to become a police officer. Unfortunately, he had not quite reached the grades he would need, and therefore in 1994 he joined the Royal Australian Navy as a mechanical engineer and would go on to see active service in East Timor and the Persian Gulf. Rich was serving aboard HMAS *Adelaide* when it was tasked to the search for missing yachtsman Tony Bullimore, who had been lost whilst competing in a single-handed around-the-world race.

With the wreckage found by the Royal Australian Air Force, all hope that Mr Bullimore had survived began to fade. The best that *Adelaide*'s crew could hope for was that they would recover the body so that his family could bury him. On arriving at the wreckage crew members used a small boat to reach it. They knocked on the hull and Mr Bullimore swam out from under his yacht. Against all odds, he had survived inside an air pocket, in total darkness and without food, for four long days. The sheer joy of the successful rescue spread throughout the crew and "morale on the ship had never been higher".

While on leave from the navy, Rich met Clare, an English woman who was backpacking around Australia. They quickly fell in love and any subsequent leave that he took would see him flying out to wherever she was staying at the time. Although she would return to England their relationship remained strong and he asked her to marry him. She accepted and flew back to Australia. After seven years in the navy, Rich left in 2001.

He and Clare were looking for a more stable life, and settled in Sydney. He took a job as an electrical water tank heater technician, and life was good for a while. It was not to last, though, as Clare missed her family dreadfully, and was never properly able to settle. Always keen to take on a new challenge, Rich relished the idea of relocating to South Yorkshire. As luck would have it, the company he was working for had offices in the UK, and he would have a job when he arrived in England.

Although having a job helped Rich find his feet and make some friends, the work was routine and offered him none of the camaraderie and discipline that he had enjoyed in the navy. He needed something that would challenge him; something a bit more exciting. It was then that he heard that South Yorkshire Police were recruiting, and his dream of being a police officer was reignited. He put in an application and following months of tests and vetting he joined the force in early 2004. To start, there were twelve weeks of residential training which took place in Harrogate in North Yorkshire. Rich's military service meant he found it easy to get to grips with the discipline and the physical side of police training. However, he acknowledges that he had to put in more effort to manage the mountains of paperwork that needed to be completed when dealing with incidents. Nonetheless, he passed every exam and could not wait to get out of training and into his first posting, and put the theory that he had been taught into practice.

He was posted to a response team at Attercliffe Police Station in Sheffield. Response officers are at the core of policing as they work revolving shifts, responding to every urgent call. After a period with a tutor constable, he was going to be walking the beat for the first six months and would be expected to "bring in three pieces of paper a day". That essentially means traffic tickets, carrying out stop searches, and giving people formal warnings for minor public order offences or low-level cannabis possession.

For an officer working in even the smallest town centre this target can be achieved relatively easily, as they are able to tackle any antisocial behaviour and drugs offences by disrupting users and dealers lurking in back alleys and darkened stairwells. They are also able to respond to incidents that have occurred nearby, including shoplifting. However, on a busy housing estate it can be virtually impossible where most offenders are getting around in vehicles or on mopeds and pushbikes and simply ignore the officer on foot as they can't usually stop or trace them. Even when he wanted to attend a live incident, it was usually just too far away to walk there before other officers were already dealing with it.

Rich found himself in a position in which he was essentially set up to fail. On the many shifts when he was unable to meet the criteria, he was warned about his performance and put under pressure to work harder. He was always working under the threat that he might not be successful in his probationary period. As his sergeant had ordered that he was not allowed to use or travel in police vehicles he couldn't even be dropped off at incident and left to deal with it. The only exception to the order was when he was on night shifts.

On those nights when he was paired up it was with a colleague who was a good friend of his sergeant, and who, instead of teaching him the job and developing his skills through constructive feedback, reported every mistake he made. It was clear to Rich that he was dealing with more than a strict supervisor: she was a bully who had taken an instant dislike to him. "When she got her teeth into me, she had me in the inspectors' office to be criticised so often that I should have had my own coffee mug." After being bullied and belittled from the beginning he started to develop a crisis of confidence, and was increasingly anxious that he would never meet the necessary standard. More important to him was he had learnt so little so far that he said, "I was concerned that I wouldn't be able to properly help and protect crime victims."

On a positive note, the fact he could work on a vehicle at night allowed him to get to know the rest of the team and to impress them with his enthusiasm and support. He destroyed any myths that he was unfit for the job. In fact, the opposite was true, and they came to see him as capable and dependable. He said, "It got to the point that each time she wrote a negative report, my colleagues would write a good one." With this support he became a highly skilled officer. He would go on to train as a public order officer including method of entry and as a chemical, biological, radiological, and nuclear (CBRN.) These officers would be at the front line if there were ever such an attack.

Soon his time on foot patrol was over and he was trained to drive immediate response vehicles. He was now a fully operational and respected member of the shift. Getting out onto the streets properly was incredible; not only was it great fun, but his confidence in his abilities grew. However, there was still so much to learn. Once Rich chased down a burglar through the backstreets and alleys, only to realise that he was lost and unable to call for backup. With his prisoner in handcuffs, "I had to walk him around until I could find a street name before I could call for a van to transport him back to the station." At some point enthusiasm will get the better of most probationers; it's almost a necessary rite of passage.

Rich was popular on his team and began building friendships that would last a lifetime. One of those was with Carl, the local police dog handler. Rich describes him as "a consummate police officer: calm, collected and very experienced. Carl always went the extra mile to support his colleagues and the public." The two officers worked well together, and their skills complemented each other, making them a formidable team. They had a great deal of success in tracking down violent offenders and securing crucial evidence. Rich saw Carl as a role model and mentor, and his example made a huge impression on him. It was devastating to Rich when Carl took his own life. Another police suicide and tragically another remarkable person lost too soon.

A police officer's own mortality is always at the back of his or her mind, as death or life-changing injury can come from anywhere in an instant. For Rich it came on a quiet Sunday afternoon, and he was patrolling with a colleague when they were sent to investigate reports of a white transit van driving dangerously at a local cemetery. The report stated that the driver was doing "doughnuts" by pulling up the handbrake while driving at high speed, so that the van swept around in a circle. Rich was in the passenger seat of a marked response car, which was driven by his colleague. Approaching the cemetery, they were driving up a steep hill. The road was narrow and lined with drystone walls and parked cars on either side. Suddenly the van came hurtling towards them, hitting the police car and sending it spinning backwards down the hill where it became wedged and stopped. Immediately Rich was out of the car and running towards the van. As he did so the driver swerved and mounted the pavement between the stone wall and the parked cars shunting them into the road. Rich said, "I reached the driver's window and tried to grab the keys. As I did that, I lost my footing and fell. The van moved forward, I was pinned between it and a parked car. I was terrified, and had no doubt that I would be crushed to death." It was sheer luck that the van stalled and when the driver restarted the engine, he reversed instead of going forward, thereby releasing Rich. "I drew my baton and tried to smash the window, but the driver was too fast and got away. I suddenly just collapsed to the floor." Rich had sustained serious injuries including deep cuts to his arms, legs and face, and his uniform trousers were torn to shreds. Dealing with people in vehicles is one of the most dangerous interactions that police officers face, and officers are regularly killed or receive life-changing injuries as a result.

Heroically, Rich limped back into work after a single day off, despite the pain that his injuries were causing him. He wanted to get back as soon as possible. "I felt guilty about being away from work and I was worried that if I didn't go back quickly then I would never be able to catch up with my outstanding paperwork. I had to be sure I was doing the best for the victims I was supporting."

He was now becoming completely overwhelmed by the amount of paperwork that resulted from him being such a proactive and conscientious officer. His first sergeant had sucked all the confidence from him with her constant criticism, and that, combined with his ADHD, meant that he was engaged in an uphill struggle from the beginning. Indeed, almost all officers are weighed down by the burden of paperwork, even when dealing with the most mundane inquiry. It must be acknowledged that police officers spend only a small proportion of their shifts actively on patrol, as every interaction or incident attended results in more paperwork. This is made far worse by the fact that many forces up and down the country still rely on outdated IT systems, which make things harder than they need to be as the various platforms often don't speak to each other which forces the officer to duplicate much of the information. It is also not uncommon for the systems to be so overwhelmed that they crash.

Consider as an example a prolific shoplifter detained by shop security. The officer dealing with the case will have a great deal of work to do to process the offence. When they arrive at the scene the first thing that they need to do is establish the facts and, if there are sufficient grounds, arrest and search the suspect. It is not unusual to wait periods of time before a van is free to transport the prisoner to custody; then booking them in and seizing and recording their property can take another hour, or an awful lot longer if the custody sergeant is already booking in another prisoner. Then it's off back to the shop to take statements and seize the CCTV footage and any other information regarding the theft. (This could be in the form of a till receipt or photographs.) Back at the station, the officer will complete an arrest statement, exhibit the evidence, and book it into the property system. A crime report will have to be completed and an intelligence report added to the system. Before even thinking about an interview, a house search must be considered if it is suspected that there may be evidence of the offence or linked crimes there. If a search is carried out and property is found, that too will be exhibited. Prior to the interview a working laptop needs to be found so that the CCTV footage can be shown to the suspect in the subsequent interview. However, if the suspect wants a solicitor, the officer is left hanging around until they turn up; then the officer must disclose the facts of the case to them and then they will want to speak to the prisoner in private.

During this time, the officer can't do anything else as they need to be ready to go as soon as the solicitor decides that they and their client are ready. Following the interview, the officer will put together a full case file before contacting the Crown Prosecution Service (CPS) for a charging decision. As there are only a limited number of CPS lawyers available at any one time this can take many hours as officers from around the country will also need advice. By now any thoughts that the officer had had about going home on time will be long gone.

It should be noted that the more serious the investigation, the more in-depth the paperwork becomes. So, for a conscientious and diligent officer like Rich, this aspect of police work would end up causing a great deal of stress and anxiety. As the welfare of his crime victims is always paramount, he was always dogged by questions when he left work. *Should I have done more? Could I have done something else? And what if?* It became so bad that the strain eventually manifested itself into tics whereby his face would tighten up and he would blink uncontrollably. Things got worse when the criminal element began to call him "blinky Bill".

At home after a shift, a glass of wine or a couple of beers was becoming the norm. Alcohol blurred the lines and gave him some respite from the anxiety. Moreover, it helped him to get to sleep. But alcohol-induced sleep leads to early waking, and the problems don't just go away. After a few hours he would be awake again and worrying as much as ever.

Back at work, on the surface at least, he was performing well and was considered a safe pair of hands. In an organisation in which promotion is based not on a person's leadership ability or merit, but instead on their ability to pass exams many supervisors are often weak and indecisive, always looking for the easy route. Consequently, it is easier to dump work onto officers like Rich who get on with it without complaining than it is to deal with those who are difficult or always ready with an excuse as to why they can't do it, or those who are just downright obstructive. Although the latter officers are in the minority, they still have a serious impact on the others who are forced to carry them.

Rich found himself in a vicious circle. More work resulted in more stress, which made it more difficult to focus and sleep. He would then abuse alcohol to knock himself out. Ultimately, it was like the film *Groundhog Day*: work, eat, sleep and repeat. "I would be coming in at four in the morning on an early shift because I had to sort out the paperwork for someone I had on bail, soon I was always the first to arrive for a shift and the last one to finish. My inspector would just have a go at me for not going home, and nobody ever asked *why* I spent so much time at work. I always put so much effort into what I did but it was never enough.

"I was becoming a functional alcoholic slipping deeper and deeper into a dark hole that I couldn't get out of." When speaking about his mental health, he said that there had been an incident years before when "I went into the inspector's office, closed the door, and I burst out crying. Over the next few weeks, I would be crying in my bedroom, the toilet, and on the way to work. The sergeant agreed a plan that if I were struggling, he would send me out of the station to get some air and then we would speak. Although positive, it was short-lived as it was not practical to maintain in the longer term." Unfortunately, it was also a missed opportunity to intervene and assist him, Rich said, "When I did try to speak to the sergeant it was impossible to explain how I was feeling as he was constantly distracted by incidents he heard on his radio or questions from other people. I know that he meant well but in the end it was pointless."

In around 2015 Rich became a tutor constable, responsible for taking an officer fresh out of training school and moulding them over twelve weeks into a knowledgeable and confident officer who can go out into the world and do the job competently and safely on their own. He enjoyed watching his charges' development. With an eye on his own early experience, he had the empathy and patience to draw the best out of people without crushing their personality or confidence. Although extremely rewarding, his new role also brought about extra stress. Rich was now responsible for the welfare of his students.

Police officers know full well that peace can descend into chaos at a moment's notice. As a tutor, keeping yourself safe comes a close second to keeping your student safe. Rich recalls doing an address check while searching for a missing person. As his student was returning to the police car, a woman ran out of a nearby house, shoeless, wearing pyjamas, and almost hysterical. It transpired that her husband, released from prison that day, had just dragged another woman into the house and up the stairs. Conscious that his student had so far struggled with confrontation, Rich cautiously led the way into the house and announced their presence, shouting, "Police officers! Show yourself!" His adrenalin was pumping as he knew that the safety of both his student and the woman inside depended on him and the actions he took. A skinny man emerged at the top of the stairs. He was holding a knife and the woman was nowhere to be seen. Rich glanced at his student, who looked terrified. Drawing his Taser he climbed the stairs, approaching the man and repeating the command, "Drop the knife!" The man backed away into a bedroom. As the officers reached the landing he reappeared, no longer holding the knife; however, he may have hidden it in a pocket. To Rich's surprise something just clicked with his student, and she took the initiative and tackled the man to the floor, arresting him. "I was so proud of her. It's amazing to watch someone who is essentially a nervous civilian transform into a confident, capable officer; someone who is going to be a great addition to the shift they later join."

Privately he was becoming more and more concerned about his drinking and knew he needed some help. "If I had gone to my sergeant, he would have had to report me to the Professional Standards Department (PSD) who would have just tried to catch me driving and do my legs." Had he believed that real help and support would be available, he would have asked for it several years before. "I was worried about the stigma and PSD becoming involved; that I might be put on light duties, or not allowed to work at all. I could have taken time off, but I was too proud and forced myself to battle through it, trying to do the best job that I could."

The grim reality is that many thousands of officers throughout the country are struggling under the enormous pressure of their workload. Almost a decade of austerity has seen cuts not only to police budgets, but to social care, mental health services, and drug and alcohol support to name just a few. As a result, agencies that would previously have been charged with those responsibilities have become increasingly unable to do so. Consequently, the police service has been forced to take on those responsibilities. As such the police struggle to cope with all of society's problems, with fewer officers and reduced resources. This impacts on every single officer. Those who are unable to cope with the workload struggle until they are completely broken down or burned out. It is little wonder that so many of them turn to alcohol as a way of coping with the unrelenting stress. Anybody can get caught up in this kind of problem; indeed, even the Queen's grandson Prince Harry admits that in the past he has turned to drugs and alcohol as a coping mechanism.

Rich was now at a stage where he desperately needed help, but had nowhere to turn. Inevitably, everything came to a head on 20th July 2019: "It was a hot summer's day, I had come off night shift and had been open-water swimming in a local reservoir with some mates from the police swim team. I was lucky to have been part of the swim team for the last twelve years. After the swim we went to the pub and had a pint before I went back home. I felt helpless and overwhelmed, so went out and bought a four-pack of 330 millilitre beers. I had a few drinks while I set up the roof box on the car as we were going to Wales the next day. My wife had gone out and I stupidly got in the car and drove to the pub, which was only four hundred metres up the road. I was really struggling and needed to switch my brain off. I had two more pints; I honestly thought that I was under the drink-drive limit, or I wouldn't have driven. I got into the car to drive home when I crashed into a small electrical box. I was mortified. I immediately went back to the pub and gave my keys to the landlord so that he could move the car. I then went home and waited for the police. I know that most people would have avoided them until they knew the alcohol was out of their system. For me, though, if I had done the wrong thing then I knew that I should face up to the consequences."

Once arrested, he was taken to the police station and breathalysed, which surprisingly confirmed that he was over the limit, at the lower level. Initially the Police Federation argued that he had mitigating circumstances and that they should be heard at the subsequent disciplinary hearing. However, it later transpired that Rich was only paying the lower level of federation subscriptions and was not entitled to legal cover. Outrageously, as of the 30th September 2019, Police Federation were sitting on £12.1 million accrued through member subscriptions; it is beyond belief that they could refuse to assist an officer in dire need. Contrast this with the fact that the six ruling members of the federation claimed £4033 for meals in January to March of 2018, the federation should exist for the benefit of the members and not for personal enrichment.

Consequently, Rich either had to pay for legal representation himself or try to fight everything alone. As he was unable to afford a lawyer, it was left to him to try to write up his mitigation and forward it to the hearing. Aware that the hearing was a formality and that the chief constable had already made the decision to dismiss him, he took the painful decision to resign. He had hoped that once he had received treatment there might still be a chance for him to rejoin the police. However, ultimately the mitigation that he had submitted was ignored and the chief constable stated that had he not resigned he would have been dismissed, and therefore his name was added to the College of Policing barred list for ten years. Therefore, he will never be a police officer again.

Although devastated by the decision, Rich remains the epitome of resilience. He didn't give up his passion for helping people and he is now a lecturer in public services at a local college. "I love what I do: I can share my experience with the next generation of police officers and properly prepare them so that they don't make the same mistakes that I did. It's not the police, but I still get some satisfaction from helping people."

Rich was a good officer with a genuine desire to do the very best he could. In doing so he struggled to manage the intense stress, and used alcohol as a crutch. He knew that he needed help, and he wanted it; unfortunately, the stigma of alcoholism coupled with the certain knowledge that the PSD would seek to act against him made it impossible for him to ask for help. In retrospect he believes that crashing his car was essentially a cry for help as he could no longer carry on with life as it was. The situation is deeply unfair, and it doesn't need to be that way.

In recent years the Baltimore Police Department has created the officer safety and wellness (OSW) section, which is "designed to advocate for the mental and physical health and wellness of both police officers and civilian staff members". The OSW looks at all aspects of the individuals mental and physical health. A key aspect of the section is the early intervention unit (EIU), which:

was created to monitor members who display potentially problematic behaviours that could (if gone unaddressed) result in disciplinary action, termination, and/or a personal crisis situation for the member. The goal of the unit is to speak with at-risk officers and get to the root cause of their issues before they become major problems. If needed, wrap-around services and resources are provided to the member. All actions taken by the EIU team are non-punitive.

Having spoken to the OSW director Vernon Herron, a man with thirty-five years of law enforcement experience, he is passionate about police well-being, and rightly proud that any employee can ask for help in the certain knowledge that they will receive it. The officer will not face any detriment to their career, and as long as they engage in the program, they are assured that no punitive action will be taken against them. A similar approach in Britain is vital if officers are ever going to receive the appropriate help when it is needed.

PC JONATHAN NICHOLAS

(NOTTINGHAMSHIRE POLICE)

At eighteen, Jonathan left his parents' home for the excitement and adventure that came with travel. He said, "I wandered the globe as a scruffy vagrant traveller, wide-eyed and fantastically naive, moving from one country to another, my passport folded over in my back pocket. That wonderful document was quite the best thing I ever possessed. It was all I needed: my ticket to freedom." For five years he travelled across Europe, Israel, Australia and finally New Zealand. Although it was something of a cliché, he was looking for something positive to do with his life; something that mattered. "Suddenly, on a fine New Zealand autumn morning in April 1983. I ran out of inspiration. At that moment, while sitting on the clean white sand of Auckland's North Shore I felt ready to return to the UK and find a career."

Back home Jonathan started running through his options. He needed a career that was challenging as well as interesting enough to sustain him throughout his working life. It was then that his brother-in-law, a special constable, handed him an application form for Nottinghamshire Police. Jonathan said, "I hadn't given the police much thought before that, other than watching *The Sweeney* on TV, thinking how cool it would be to charge around with my mates in a Ford Consul with a gun in my pocket." Deciding he had nothing to lose, he applied.

His training began in February 1984. His scruffy clothes were swapped for a uniform, the tunic emblazoned with silver buttons bearing an image of the crown. The long hair and straggly beard were gone too, as he now sported a short back and sides and a neatly trimmed moustache. Although he looked different, he was still the same person with the same spirit of adventure and couldn't wait to embark on his career.

By the time he passed out of training the miners' strike had become bitterly entrenched, with both the government and the National Union of Mineworkers refusing to concede anything to the other. As Nottinghamshire had several mines, local policing was spread extremely thinly. To maintain order, officers were drafted in from forces all over the country to support those struggling to contain the strike. In those days Jonathan would have learnt the job by walking a beat in the company of a tutor constable as the slower pace of life meant that an officer had significantly more opportunity to deal with crime. It was very different to what Rich would have experienced. Instead, they were responding to incidents in a car. They would work a ten-day stretch of twelve-hour shifts and then have a single day off.

At work it was so busy that they spent their days racing from one incident to another. "It wasn't long before I was completely exhausted. That said I wasn't learning very much either as all we could do was "cuff" jobs (write them off without any further action) as there was absolutely no time to investigate them, even if there were positive lines of inquiry. We wanted to provide a better service to people, but there were so few of us it was literally impossible because there would be another job to attend before you had even finished the last." Had they done anything else they would have become so bogged down with work that the whole system would soon have come to a crashing halt.

Occasionally he was taken off response and posted onto a police minibus. They were there as a reserve to be called in if any strikes became violent. "We would sit around all day in a smoky vehicle with a strong odour of flatulence, drinking pop and eating plastic sandwiches. There was nothing much else to do except take the piss out of one another." These long days of boredom were sometimes punctuated by a call for backup at some far distant pit. Unlike today, where police vehicles are covered in reflective livery and state-of-the-art blue lights and sirens, at that time the only thing that differentiated the police minibus was a slowly revolving rooftop bulb. Therefore, any high-speed blue light run would be both heart-stopping and dangerous as they weaved in and out of traffic and crossed busy junctions. When they did eventually arrive at the scene, invariably peace had already been restored, and they were no longer needed.

The strike finally came to an end in the spring of the following year, and Nottinghamshire returned to ordinary policing. As Jonathan hadn't completed his two-year probationary period he was required to get out on the beat and generate his own work so that he could be signed off as being competent in the role. Initially Jonathan found this side of policing difficult, which could only be expected as he was only taught how to "cuff" a job instead of investigating it. Naturally it wasn't long before his sergeant was breathing down his neck and demanding that he justify his existence if he was to successfully complete his probation.

Taking the criticism on board Jonathan relied on the advice and support from his colleagues and quickly got to grips with what he was doing, and he took pride in being a conscientious and caring officer. His hard work paid off and he was confirmed in rank. However, he was then back behind the wheel and responding to incidents. "I was still a relatively new cop, so I did what was expected of me, I kept my head down and got on with my job." But after ten years of the relentless demand, I was burned out and exhausted. Sometimes I was so overwhelmed that I found myself crying into the steering wheel of my police car. Something had to give."

It is impossible for any human being to sustain that level of constant pressure for a prolonged period, particularly as policing is extremely unpredictable. Jonathan could go from comforting an elderly burglary victim to a scene of utter horror and devastation in a matter of minutes; these incidents of mindless violence and abuse can shock an officer to their very core. The savagery that a human being is capable of inflicting on another is just incredible, and it is something that police officers face all too regularly.

An example came early in his service when he was called to a domestic disturbance. A woman had reported that her partner was drunk and abusive and armed with weapons. She was afraid for her safety and that of her children. When Jonathan and his colleagues arrived, the man inside the house could be heard singing songs glorifying Hitler. As Jonathan was trained in public order, he and two other officers were ordered to enter the property with riot shields and secure the unstable man. "The plan was that a colleague would put the door in so that we could rush in and get him. The element of surprise was lost as it took four heavy strikes of the Enforcer (a short, handheld battering ram) to break down the door. We could hear that the man inside was becoming angrier all the time, and his threats of violence were more vivid than ever. Once we got inside the house, we moved to the living-room door, where we could see him in the middle of the room. He was almost rabid, snarling and screaming at us. We were up against a neo-Nazi armed with a homemade spear (a broom handle with a knife taped to the end) and a large machete. The situation couldn't have been more dangerous." The living-room furniture was smashed to pieces and there was debris all over the floor. Moving into the room so that they could secure the man, they had to be careful not to trip or fall.

To do so would leave them vulnerable to attack and possible death. Several years earlier during the Broadwater Farm riot in London, that is exactly what had happened to PC Keith Blakelock. After falling, he was stabbed and hacked to death. With that memory still fresh in the minds of Jonathan and his colleague, it took great courage for them to control their fear and charge at the man, pushing him back against a wall and holding him there with their shields so that he could be disarmed and arrested. In recognition of his efforts that day, Jonathan was awarded a chief constable's commendation for bravery.

By 1995, crime was soaring out of control and the police were so overwhelmed that it had become impossible for them to attend every incident and take a crime report. To address this issue, Nottinghamshire Police created the "crime desk". The plan was that officers would now take reports of low-level crime over the phone instead of sending an officer to the scene. In serious need of respite from the stress of response policing, Jonathan applied and joined the team. Initially the job was exactly what he needed. He was one of five officers who were able to complete the four-page crime report in good time whilst still providing the victim with a quality service. Things changed when the force moved away from recording reports on paper. For officers who had been unwilling to use typewriters it was a massive culture shock when computers and information technology systems were introduced, particularly as there had been no training due to an assumption that people would know how to use them.

In truth the officers had to rely on each other and muddle through, and often simple tasks were made extremely difficult. As well as reporting every new crime, the team were required to input all the previous paper crime reports onto the system. As a result, their workload spiralled out of control and Jonathan went from dealing with an average of six crimes a day to around fifty. "I was at the end of my tether; I was again completely and utterly exhausted, and I just couldn't cope with it any longer. Then I had what I can only describe as a breakdown in late July or early August 2001, and had to go on sick leave.

"I was diagnosed with stress and anxiety. I started having counselling. Originally occupational health had suggested that I would need to have six one-hour sessions; however, they quickly realised that I needed more. In the end I had eight two-hour sessions." It is little wonder that he got to this point, as in the previous year he had personally dealt with 2,730 crimes.

When Jonathan returned to work six weeks later, he didn't return to the crime desk; instead, he was moved to a quieter area of the force where he would become a local beat officer. "This was a good move for me as I was working with very experienced officers. I was paired up with someone until I found my feet and my confidence began to return." He enjoyed not driving a police car everywhere or being stuck behind a desk as he had been for the first seventeen years of his career. "I loved it. I attended a problem-solving course, and it seemed like I might get to do some good in community policing."

Just when it seemed like he could settle down and get stuck into his new role, the rug was pulled from under him. Nottinghamshire Police had decided to move people around and centralise their resources, which in layman's terms meant that officers were shuffled all around the area the force covered. Jonathan ended up back where he had started: in a car and responding to incidents. As such, there was a very real possibility that his mental health would deteriorate once again. Therefore, he kept his eye out for a new role. Then he learned that the Criminal Investigation Department (CID) was looking for a uniformed officer to join them on a burglary initiative. Jonathan applied and was successful. It proved to be a great move and he thoroughly enjoyed the work: following up on every report of a burglary, looking for further evidence and identifying the offenders. When he found anything, the detectives would take over and make the arrest. The team were becoming successful, too successful for police leaders, who often abandon their last vestiges of logic and common sense in their pursuit of promotion. "Perhaps we should have been less successful, because when the number of burglaries went down our team was quickly disbanded and the resources shifted elsewhere, so that the next person could be promoted on the back of other people's efforts."

This obviously caused some anxiety for the officers involved, as they could technically be put into any role anywhere in the force's area. Jonathan was lucky enough to be offered a neighbourhood beat manager's role in the north of the city. His new area was unusual as it included a large hospital and two large residential estates. Undeterred by the enormity of the work that lay ahead, he immediately got stuck into his new role.

"Crime in the hospital was extremely high, with seventy to one hundred offences reported each month." As such, he took time to get to know the hospital's security staff. He passed on his mobile phone number so that they could call him to come and deal with anything criminal or suspicious if he was on duty at the time. If he wasn't he would personally follow it up when he returned. Soon his commitment and hard work paid off when he identified and arrested a habitual thief. At the time the offender had racked up 126 convictions.

However, despite receiving further convictions he was released instead of being sent to prison. As can only be expected he continued to commit crime on the hospital campus with Jonathan arresting him several more times. It was only by thinking outside the box that Jonathan was able to stop this walking crime wave. It turned out that he was illegally subletting his flat and he was evicted and moved away from the area.

One residential area on Jonathan's patch was a large, tough council estate plagued by high crime levels and controlled by organised criminals. At his first tenants' meeting, Jonathan was inspired by how hard many of the residents were working to improve the estate; not only for their own benefit, but also for their neighbours. Indeed, one lady had selflessly volunteered to open and close the community centre every day so that various local groups could use the space; moreover, she had done so for many years. Jonathan built strong relationships with the residents that were based on mutual trust and respect, and he couldn't wait to get stuck in and help them.

In an early initiative, he secured a small grant. As he was a drummer, he used the money to buy a drum kit and set up a music club in the community centre for the local kids and young people. At first, only one or two kids turned up. Nevertheless, Jonathan persevered, and he would always be at the club when it was open to teach the kids how to play. To move the club forward, he applied for a further grant from the local council so that he could provide additional equipment. He was successful, and used the money to purchase a guitar and a piano. As both his teenage sons were able to play these instruments, they would come to the club so that the kids could learn how to play them. Jonathan ran the club for two hours every Tuesday and Thursday. He did so while off duty and in his own time. The music club grew quickly and soon up to thirty-five young people were attending. Which was a great achievement as they were off the streets and in a safe environment. Mindful that many of them lived in poverty and might not have eaten before the session, Jonathan would always bring along bags of bananas so that they would at least have a healthy snack. He went above and beyond what was reasonably expected of him for the benefit of the community. It was while talking to him he inadvertently let slip that he had been buying the snacks himself.

The local council were so impressed by what he had achieved that they allocated a youth worker to assist him. By getting to know the young people, Jonathan soon got to know their parents and became a well-known figure on the estate and as such he got to know the residents well and he was able to address their concerns. Talking to people and gaining their confidence meant that they would tell him about some of the more serious crime on the estate. Though they would never have contacted the police directly, now at least Jonathan could pass on the information to his colleagues, who were able to resolve the problem. It wasn't long therefore before crime and antisocial behaviour on the estate plummeted.

Most of the music club's members worked extremely hard and were learning numerous instruments. Unfortunately, no matter how well they were doing, it was still clear to Jonathan that they had extremely low aspirations. One day he asked them what they would do if they won the lottery, and was saddened to hear that the best dream they came up with was to buy the biggest caravan in Skegness. To broaden their horizons, Jonathan and the kids formed a band which they called "Convicted", which is ironic as there was not a conviction among them. It wasn't long before the band were on the move and doing gigs around the city. Jonathan used a large, liveried prisoner van as a gig bus and Convicted would even appear at the Sherwood Festival for three years in a row.

Jonathan ran the music club by recognising and rewarding good behaviour. He would allow the young people to take home the instruments and amplifiers. His intention was to build their confidence and self-esteem by showing them that they had earned his trust and respect. On one occasion he managed to get hold of tickets for a live concert at Wembley Stadium, and took three youngsters down in his own car. "It was amazing to watch them take everything in. The music club ran for seven years, and it was incredible to see the kids grow in confidence and begin to realise that life didn't start and stop on the estate."

His dedication to the community was having a significant impact, crime on the estate was down and he was diverting more and more young residents away from trouble. Consequently, trust and respect between the residents and the police improved greatly. In 2007 Jonathan was named Beat Manager of the Year by Nottinghamshire Police. The best beat managers from around the country were then invited to London to meet the then Prime Minister, Tony Blair. Jonathan said, "I went down to London with my wife; it was a cool event and I got as pissed as a fart." The following year he was again invited to London to meet Blair again, as he was among the 250 most inspirational officers in the country.

Although it was good to be recognised for his achievements, the work of a police officer never ceases and there were still investigations to complete and offenders to lock up. Jonathan was getting a lot of job satisfaction, particularly seeing several young people move on from his music club to study at the Music Academy in Nottingham. His intervention and hard work had given them the opportunity to have an incredible future.

Jonathan's creative talents went beyond just music as he was also a keen writer who had kept a journal from a very young age. He regularly had letters published in police magazines. This led an editor to offer him the opportunity to write his own column, for doing so he would be paid a nominal fee. As he was a serving officer, he couldn't do this until he had gained consent from the professional standards department, which he duly received. Writing the column proved to be an enjoyable experience and, as he now had official permission to be a writer, he began to write a book based on his experiences at the hospital. *Hospital Beat* was published in 2011 and was described by its publisher as "weird, shocking, moving and often amusing". In the book Jonathan celebrated all the successes which he had achieved at the hospital, highlighting the excellent working relationship that he had with the staff, particularly the security team. "I thought the book showed Nottinghamshire Police in a positive light, so I sent a copy to the PR department to see if they were interested." Although most people liked it, a civilian member of staff forwarded it to the PSD.

Then, towards the middle of 2012, he was contacted by the PSD, who served him with papers stating that he had failed to gain permission to write the book, and, as this amounted to gross misconduct if found guilty, he could be sacked from the police. Jonathan was astounded as he believed he *had* been given permission to be a writer. However, as it turned out the whole investigation was based on semantics as he was only permitted to be a "columnist", not a "writer in general". Despite it being a simple and obvious mistake, the PSD pushed forward.

Then, while already on the verge of losing everything, the PSD reappeared and served him with a further set of papers. This time he was being investigated regarding his handling of an allegation of sexual assault. Again, this amounted to gross misconduct. After twenty eight and a half years of unblemished service, he stood on the verge of losing everything that he had worked his entire life to achieve. It is little wonder then that his mental health began to deteriorate.

It took him some time before he realised where the second complaint could have come from. Then he remembered a woman whom he had dealt with on several occasions. He had first met her when he'd gone to her address to investigate concerns about the welfare of her children. Once there, he discovered that the children were severely neglected and living in squalid conditions. The only course of action he could take was to remove them from her custody and take them into police protection, from which they were placed in the care of social services. On a separate occasion he had arrested her for throwing a rock through the front window of her parents' house. In the interview that followed she denied everything until she was shown CCTV footage that proved her guilt. She then became angry and said, "I only did it because he (her father) had sexually abused me." Jonathan immediately addressed that assertion, reassuring her that, "As soon as we finish this interview, I will take you upstairs to the sexual offences unit, where they can investigate the allegation." In fact, he had said the same thing on three separate occasions.

Following the interview, he'd done everything possible to convince her to speak to the officers in the sexual offence's unit; however, she'd made feeble excuses and left the police station. It is worth noting that she had made no subsequent attempt to either call the police or return to the station to report the offence.

Now she had complained that Jonathan had failed to investigate the allegation she had made against her father. To be perfectly clear, the PSD was not alleging that he had failed in his duty to investigate her allegation as it was not in his remit to do so. The investigation was related solely to the fact that he had failed to submit a crime report, as he knew no details of the allegation the report would essentially have been blank. Now as the interview had been recorded Jonathan reasonably believed that the PSD would listen to the tape and hear that he had done everything he possibly could to assist the complainant and the allegation would be dismissed.

That did not happen and for a long time, the two investigations overlapped. When the PSD eventually interviewed him about his book, they again reasserted the threat that he was likely to be dismissed. The pressure on Jonathan was intense as he risked losing so much. "I just couldn't believe it; I was so close to retiring and I was about to lose everything. I ended up in floods of tears and I think in the end they maybe thought I had shown the right amount of contrition. When the investigation was finally over, it was dispensed with by a recommendation of management advice, which is the lowest sanction possible."

The malicious complaint, however, lingered on for eighteen months. All the time, Jonathan was in a state of purgatory as he drew closer to a retirement that potentially lay in ruins. Throughout the investigation he received various letters from the PSD, though they were inconsistent, as some stated the allegation amounted to gross misconduct and others as misconduct. For Jonathan, he had no idea where he stood, and he was forced to chase the PSD for an answer. "It was like banging my head against a brick wall."

It is scandalous that the PSD took so long to complete their investigation. Jonathan said, "It was an awful time. I felt paranoid as I hadn't done anything to justify the investigations. I was not getting any joy out of life, and I was unable to look forward to the future. I just couldn't understand it when people were laughing in the office, I really could not see anything that was funny. I didn't believe I had a way out and thought all my life's work would disappear, so I seriously contemplated stepping into traffic in my uniform." In the end, he had a breakdown and was not able to return to work.

When he was interviewed about the second allegation, the PSD officers still couldn't decide whether they were treating the allegation as gross misconduct or misconduct. The irony of them failing to record things correctly was not lost on Jonathan. The PSD browbeat him relentlessly for failing to record a crime report following what had essentially been a throwaway comment; albeit it remained clear that he had done everything in his power to help the woman. The interrogation of Winston Smith in George Orwell's book *1984* has never been more evident.

In the last two weeks of his service, he was instructed to report to the superintendent. It had again been decided to dispense with the complaint by way of "management advice". This was to be delivered during the meeting. On arrival Jonathan was not given a chance to speak as the man tore a strip off him, demanding that he not make the same mistake in the future. Jonathan let him get it all off his chest before informing him that he would be retiring in just over a week. Exasperated the superintendent screwed up the paperwork, threw it in the bin and told him to leave.

After he had retired, Jonathan wrote a second book *Who'd Be a Copper?* It was a cathartic experience and helped him with his recovery, and it was the last thing he did involving the police until he contributed to this book. He said, "It has taken a long time to get better." But although he has found it difficult to go through his past to tell this story he ends by saying, "It will be worth it if it helps others in a similar situation."

SERGEANT "ANNA"
(MIDLANDS)

'Anna' (not her real name as she wants to keep her anonymity) had been a police officer for six years when she was seriously assaulted. She recalled, "We responded to an emergency call about a fight in a shop. When we arrived, we found that the place had been smashed up and there was stuff all over the floor. The suspect had gone but the victim had been badly assaulted as the suspect had hit him with one of the metal shelves. When the victim had been taken to the hospital my shift partner went back to the station to get the case file started and I stayed and waited for the CSI.

"I was inside the shop with the CSI when I heard shouting outside. When I went out, I saw two men arguing. One of them told me that the other had been 'having a go' at the CSI van. I chased him into the back alleys while calling for assistance on the radio. It was late afternoon in November and as it was already dark, I lost him. I decided to go back to the shop and let the responding officers do an area search.

"I hadn't been back more than a few minutes when there was another disturbance outside. The suspect was back again, and this time he had a crowbar and was smashing up the van. A member of the public pointed at the alley where the suspect was running away.

So, I chased after him again. When I came out of the alley onto a street of terraced houses, I could see the suspect on the other side of the street a little bit ahead of me; he was walking and laughing to himself. I crossed the street and called for him to stop, but he just told me to 'fuck off' and ran away laughing. I again called for assistance and chased him up to a crossroads and saw him climb into the front garden of a house. The garden was surrounded by a wall and a high fence.

"I climbed over and drew my extendable baton as I was concerned that he still had the crowbar. The garden was so small, and I could see he was now only a few feet ahead of me, trying to climb a trellis into the next garden. The trellis gave way and he landed on his feet. I told him to lay on the floor so that I could handcuff him. Instead, he picked up the heavy side of the wooden trellis, which had jagged nails sticking out of it, and hit me on the side of my body. I caught hold of the wood with my left hand before he could hit me again, and I struck him across the hip with my baton. I had planned to strike him across the thigh, but he was so much taller than me. The strike seemed to have no effect on him, and he just ripped the baton out of my hand and pushed me backwards. I tripped on a tree root and fell, so that my shoulders were wedged between the tree and the fence. He then jumped straight onto my legs, stopping me from getting away from him.

"I reached for my radio to let my colleagues know where I was, but it was missing and must have been lost during the initial struggle. I was terrified and convinced that he was going to kill me, as he raised my baton above his head. I was trapped, and he was physically much stronger and heavier than me. I'm only five foot four and weigh seven and a half stone. Before he could hit me, I managed to get my CS spray off my utility belt, and I sprayed him in the face. Again, this barely fazed him. He pulled the can from my hand and threw it away before twice punching me full force in the face.

He got up and threw away my baton before trying to get over the fence again. I managed to get myself up and scrambled around, trying to find my baton in the dark. That's when I heard the police sirens. I was screaming and waving my baton, hoping that they would see or hear me. The man then stopped and turned back to me. I struck him several times, trying to keep him away. It's crazy; I was in fear for my life, but I was still very careful not to hit his head because I feared the consequences of being sent to prison if he was injured. He pushed me aside and jumped back over the fence he had used to get in the garden. He virtually landed at the feet of the officers backing me up. Even then he didn't give up, and during the struggle he assaulted three of them.

"I later found out how lucky I had been. It turns out the officers hadn't seen me and were driving past when a member of the public flagged them down and pointed out where the screaming was coming from. I dread to think what would have happened if they had passed by and I had been trapped alone with the man." You might assume that such a violent man would receive a substantial prison sentence. Unfortunately, that was not the case, as once again the CPS and courts let the victims down, sentencing him to prison for just eighteen months.

Anna was treated for severe bruising and spent the rest of the week recovering at home before returning to work. "I thought that I was fine, but I wasn't, and things only got worse. I was angry all the time, I couldn't handle loud noises, and I had no patience any more for other people. I wasn't sleeping well, and I was relying on alcohol so much that I was putting myself at risk, but I didn't care. I just wanted to stop feeling the way that I did. It would work for a while, but it never lasted. I found that I couldn't even talk about what had happened, and I was self-harming by punching walls. I would go to the gym, trying to get the anger out of my system, but even that didn't help. I was having flashbacks of the incident and my heart felt like it was beating out of my chest, which was making me even more angry and anxious. I hated it. I couldn't sit still, I couldn't focus, and tasks that I would normally complete quickly were taking me ages to finish. About two months after the incident, I went to see my sergeant and broke down. I couldn't carry on the way that I was as I was exhausted and knew that something was wrong."

Anna's sergeant told her to report sick; however, that would have been the worst situation for her as she would have had too much time to ruminate. She felt that she needed the distraction of work to help her to come to terms with what had happened. Although she wasn't forced to stay, she was taken off response and posted to the prisoner handling team, where she would interview prisoners and prepare court files. At the same time, her force arranged for her to have six sessions of counselling through occupational health, and she was diagnosed with PTSD.

As her mental health improved, she started going out to attend pre-arranged appointments. After around six months she returned to response policing. On her first shift she was patrolling alone when reports of a suspected drug dealer came into the control room, and Anna took the job. On arrival she approached the man, who was acting "shifty", and attempted to detain him in her car until a male colleague could search him. The man resisted and assaulted her, pushing her across the bonnet of the police car before running away. Back at the station, while Anna was writing up her statement her sergeant came in and told her that he didn't believe that she had been assaulted on her first day back on response, and that she was exaggerating what had happened. He only accepted the truth after seeing the incident, which, fortunately, had been captured on CCTV. It is an example of the underlying misogyny that still exists in some male police officers.

Anna was twenty-one when she joined the police, that said, she already had some experience as she had been a special constable for several months. However, "Because I was young, short in stature and very slight, I initially had a bit of an issue where a couple of my male colleagues would step in and take over while I was dealing with incidents. Although their intentions were good, I had to speak to them, explaining that they were undermining my authority and abilities, which as a woman made my job even more difficult. They took it on board and quickly realised that I could take care of myself. What I didn't have in bulk I more than made up for as I'm feisty and gobby." It is these attributes that have always inspired the respect and admiration of her colleagues.

It is, therefore, no surprise that by March 2020 she was promoted to acting sergeant, even though at that time she had still not completed her sergeant's exam. She was posted to a relatively inexperienced team and soon proved her worth when in October she arrived to back up and supervise her colleagues who were dealing with an incident in which two young women had been hit by a train. The scene that she encountered was truly horrendous: an eighteen-year-old girl was trapped under the train and already dead, while her seventeen-year-old friend was being treated by police and paramedics at the back of the train. The girls had been drinking with friends in a field near to the approach to the station, and had been hit on a level crossing. Although the British Transport Police have the responsibility for policing the rail network and its infrastructure, it was Anna and her team who arrived first. She had led from the front, ensuring that immediate first aid was under way, that the scene was secure, and that the evidence that would form the basis of a serious investigation was secured. When the BTP sergeant arrived he was completely out of his depth and he constantly sought reassurance and direction from Anna, which made her job even more difficult. In the wake of the incident, she proved herself to be an extremely compassionate supervisor who put her team's welfare above her own.

In the days that followed, though, Anna began to realise that she was again not herself. Usually loud and happy, she had become introverted and was again having trouble sleeping. She was also having flashbacks in which she saw the girl trapped under the train. As she arrived at work for a night shift, the sergeant from whom she was taking over noticed that she was not herself and he asked if she wanted to talk about it. Anna would again be diagnosed with PTSD and undergo another period of counselling. However, her colleague would be her rock and he supported her throughout, and they are now very close friends.

In May 2021 her team dealt with another horrific incident. In the preceding weeks, a woman had called the police regularly, reporting that her ex-partner was coming to her address and hanging around the garden; an activity which escalated to him causing some damage. One night when Anna was covering another part of the force two of her officers responded to the woman's latest call. The officers searched the garden and took a statement before leaving with the intention of arresting the man. However, unknown to them he had been hiding under a barbecue cover. Once the officers had gone the woman went into the garden for a cigarette, at which point her abuser emerged and attacked her.

A neighbour called the police after hearing screaming, and the two officers returned to the house and found the man straddling the woman, strangling her. The first officer to enter the garden had just over two years' service, he tried to pull the man off. His colleague then entered and was able to incapacitate the man with her Taser. Without it they would have struggled, as the man was much bigger and stronger than they were. With the man restrained they began first aid for the victim, which was a gruesome task as she had also been stabbed twenty-one times, many of them to the face. Unfortunately, she would die two weeks later whilst still in intensive care. The officers were left deeply traumatised.

The entire incident had been recorded on their body cameras and, being the empathetic and caring supervisor that she was, Anna put their needs above hers and watched the footage. She needed to know exactly what they had been through so that she could properly support them. The selflessness she demonstrated at a time when her own PTSD was so raw is incredible, and it is what made her such an amazing supervisor.

Anna was becoming increasingly anxious for another reason; the sergeant's promotion boards were approaching in September. Not only had she always struggled with interviews her PTSD was very debilitating at the time. She explained to me how the nerves had got the better of her in the past when she had applied for the fraud squad. Her previous experience made her an exceptional candidate for the role. Fraud is a very difficult aspect of policing, and something that many officers shy away from due to the complexity of the investigations. But as Anna was known for her diligence and interest in the area, she was tasked with attending a report which suggested that an elderly lady had been defrauded of £75,000. Anna retained the inquiry and investigated the case for almost two years and built an exceptional case against the defendant, which led to them being found guilty in court. The prosecuting barrister was so impressed by Anna that she emailed her supervisor and superintendent, stating:

She is indeed as thorough as you have said, [name redacted]. From the little that I have seen of her, she is bright, has a good memory and is well organised. She should have been the OIC (officer in charge) in our fraud as she started it off in the force. I feel that her talent and the rare quality of being thorough and careful with paperwork is wasted in the response unit when her preference is for investigating fraud (most officers hate them and have no clue what to do and are not half as assiduous in their paperwork preparation as she was).

Despite her obvious extraordinary talent, Anna was unsuccessful in her interview for the fraud squad as her anxiety about the interview was so high that it triggered her PTSD leaving her extremely tired, confused, and unable to express herself and display her qualities. With the promotions board looming, she began looking for all the help that she could get, including speaking to colleagues who have previously passed the boards for advice or tips. In preparation, Anna said, "I spoke to everyone and anyone who I thought might be able to advise me, including a civilian who sits on the interview board as he may have some old questions I could use. A couple of days later that person sent me a list of what I thought were example questions via text message. By that time, though, I was being mentored by an inspector who I had known since I was a special constable. I sent him the questions via my police mobile. However, as we didn't use them in my mock interviews, I forgot all about them."

When the date of the boards finally arrived, Anna had to complete several exercises and then ten minutes before the interview she was given the questions she would be asked. With her anxiety at its peak, she didn't realise that they were the same questions that she had previously received via text. Regardless of that her responses in the interview relied on the examples that she had already used in her application form.

In the days that followed she reflected and began to realise that she had received the interview questions in advance via text message. Anna prides herself on her integrity and immediately contacted her inspector to report what had happened. They had been good friends for several years, and that may have been the reason why the inspector took a couple of days before she advised Anna to report the matter to the PSD. When Anna returned to work the PSD were waiting for her and served her with papers stating that she was under investigation based on the following standards of behaviour:

1. Honesty and integrity.
2. Orders and instructions.

3. Confidentiality.
4. Discreditable conduct.
5. Duties and responsibilities.

Anna was stunned as she had not done anything wrong. Despite what had happened she maintained her composure and attempted to finish her shift; however, eventually she had to go home as she was unable to concentrate. The following day she returned to work and discovered that her temporary promotion was being terminated and she was being reverted to the rank of constable. She was moved from the response team to a neighbourhood team, where she was tasked with reducing the number of outstanding incidents. She was ordered not to communicate with her inspector and her mentor, who was now also under investigation. Although she was under a great deal of pressure, she remained professional and worked extremely hard.

Within three weeks of the promotions board, she was interviewed by the PSD. "I was grilled for almost two hours; they constantly asked me the same questions. It was like they thought they were going to catch me out on a lie. It was a horrible experience and I spent most of the time crying. I just told them the truth over and over. At the end I thought that they now had everything they needed to finish the investigation. I was holding out a bit of hope as my fed rep had told me that I would receive a final written warning, as there was an inspector in a southern force who was warned after making a similar mistake."

Instead, Anna was called in for another interview. This time, she said, "They were more aggressive than before, claiming that I was a liar as I deliberately sought out the questions and I knew that they were correct, and that they were sent to my personal phone so that nobody would find out. That was ridiculous because I had forwarded them to my mentor on my police phone, and told him where they had come from. The fact is that I had nothing to hide because its common knowledge that everything you do on the phones is recorded and accessible. The fact is, I *did not* ask for the questions, and when I got the text, I honestly believed they were examples of the type of thing I might be asked. The problem was that they just wouldn't listen to what I was saying, and they were getting increasingly snarky and argumentative. It was one of the worst experiences of my life and I wanted to walk out. The only thing that stopped me was the knowledge that if I did, they would just drag me back in for another interview.

"After the interviews I found out that they were going to proceed with an accelerated hearing led by the chief constable. This meant that the PSD would write up the investigation and the chief constable would hold a hearing where I could attend. In the end I didn't, because my fed rep had spoken to the chief beforehand to see if he could get an indication of what may happen. It turned out that the chief had already made up his mind as he apparently wanted 'to make an example of me' and I would be fired. Therefore, my fed rep advised me to resign. I resigned from the force on New Year's Eve 2021. It was heartbreaking; I had loved my job and my team, and I was now going to start the New Year unemployed."

To read Anna's character references is to read about an inspirational and dedicated officer who was extremely well regarded. In one, a sergeant who had supervised her back in 2012 said:

"I would describe her as the mother of the shift. As well as doing her own work she would take others under her wing. She would take time to sit down with other officers and make sure that they understood what they needed to do. She was approachable and never turned people away who needed her advice. I work a flexible shift pattern and sometimes I'm in slightly later than the rest of the shift. Although she was not the longest serving member of the shift she stepped

up and quickly became proficient in the shift handover. She would competently allocate jobs and prisoners and she had the respect of the shift to do so. By the time that I arrived, everything had been sorted and was running smoothly."

In another reference, one of her sergeants wrote:

"I found [Anna] to be a very capable officer who, although not that experienced, wasn't afraid to make decisions whilst taking all factors into account. She says it as it is, she is direct and doesn't mince her words, but not rude or abrupt and this attitude endeared her to people, as more often than not they were thinking exactly the same thing. She is a tutor and her ability to give clear direct instruction helped her students a lot. By being a keen, enthusiastic officer who is hard-working she provided a high benchmark for her students."

When she was a temporary sergeant, officers from Anna's team had made an arrest following an incident of domestic violence. In short, the custody sergeant had refused to book the prisoner into custody, instead asserting that he should be sectioned under the Mental Health Act. I now quote from a performance record of the incident:

"Whilst officers were at [name of the custody station redacted] with the suspect [Anna] coordinated the response to custody's refusal – contacting public protection, the mental health team, organising triage [Anna] showed incredible tenacity, determination, and great resilience in a very difficult situation. She fought for what was right, not just for the injured party (which is vitally important and shows clear community and customer focus)[,] but also for the force (showing strategic perspective) with regards

to the correct way to deal with high-risk domestic violence incidents and knife-enabled offences – two issues that heavily affect public perception and confidence in the police[,] and for her officers – showing strong leadership and decision-making and not backing down from what she believes in."

Another character reference stated:

"I have known [Anna] on and off for several years, and I would say since 2019 I have got to know her very well and we have become friends. I have got to know [Anna] more by working alongside her as a sergeant at [station name redacted] and by doing so I have been able to make a very good friend, whom I have been able to support and who has supported me through some of the harder aspects of being a police officer. As an example, I supported [Anna] after she attended an incident where some teenagers were hit by a train causing death to one and serious injuries to another. I saw in those times how good an officer she was, when as a temporary sergeant, she dealt with this incident with the utmost competency and professionalism, which was reflected in the feedback she received. However, I also saw how much she cares, and I supported her as she was in tears on numerous occasions after that incident due to the significant impact that it had on her. This is the mark of the woman who in times of adversity, pressure, and emotional turmoil still puts others before herself and remains professional despite how she is feeling inside."

It is abundantly clear that Anna was an excellent police officer who was passionate about serving her community while leading from the front and ensuring the welfare of her team. Ultimately, she was penalised for her honesty and integrity, as she could have said nothing about the text message containing the interview questions and thereby retained her job.

For her career to be lost in this way is a significant loss to the force, the public and her colleagues have also all lost out. She is brave, compassionate, and extremely hard-working. In truth, she would never have found herself in this situation had it not been for her PTSD and the overwhelming stress that she was under. In fact, officers she used to supervise still contact her for advice and support. Anna now has a job in the insurance industry and her new employers have already noticed her talents, as within weeks of her being there she was asked if she would consider a promotion.

PC PAUL MCVEIGH

(NORTHUMBRIA POLICE)

Paul grew up in the North-East of England, which has a strong seafaring and shipbuilding tradition, dating back centuries. Like many young people in the region, he held an ambition to join the Royal Navy as a marine engineer. As a young man he was a competitive swimmer who regularly represented Washington Amateur Swimming Club in the butterfly and individual medley. When not swimming he was a keen Scout who loved camping and the outdoors. After his O Levels, he stayed on at sixth form college and briefly studied for A Levels in maths, chemistry, and physics. However, he was soon bored, and fed up with having no money. He was desperate to get a job so that he could learn to drive and buy a car.

Initially he took a clerical job with Newcastle City Council and joined the Royal Naval Reserve as a marine engineer mechanic. During his basic training he won the coveted Best New Entry award. Although being in the reserves would already help him to prepare for his enlistment, he wanted to gain even more experience so that he could move up the ranks quickly. Therefore, he left the council and moved into a sales role specialising in pumps and motors and then non-ferrous metals.

The next couple of years passed in a flash, and at twenty-one Paul was in a serious relationship and his partner was pregnant. His priorities shifted, and he made the decision that he could no longer join the Royal Navy as it was important for him to be fully involved in the baby's life and he could not do that when he was at sea for months on end. He said, "We struggled financially, as a lot of young families do, so I looked at new career options. I needed something that would give us a solid financial base." Although he had grown up knowing a handful of police officers until now, he had never considered the job for himself. "I had an uncle who had served a couple of years, then left, to go back to work in the shipyards, and a few of our neighbours were police officers and they all seemed like decent people. One of my friends' dad was a police officer and he was someone we all looked up to as kids. He would tell us stories of what it was like on the Special Patrol Group during the 1970s and 1980s. He said that the team were a close-knit group, like it had been in the Royal Marines. I joined because it seemed like a decent job and a reasonable replacement for the military.

"I joined Northumbria Police in April 1992, aged twenty-two. The physical side was tough to begin with, although the swimming test was easy, but the job just clicked with me, and I got to grips with it quickly." It was almost a surprise to him how much he enjoyed the work; more than that, though, he was extremely good at it and quickly earned the trust of his supervisors and peers. In just over a year, he had his driving authority and was out on independent patrol. "It was a brilliant feeling, and I was eager to get going." His experience and confidence grew with each new incident, and he was confident that he could deal with most things. However, he was about to be tested like he had never been before.

Late in the winter of 1993, Paul was working alone when he was tasked to deal with a "concern for welfare" at Jarrow Metro Station, where there were reports of a man collapsed. On arrival he found the man sprawled across the platform. He was alive and smelled strongly of alcohol. Paul nudged him awake and attempted to help him up. As he did so, the man threw a haymaker of a punch, hitting Paul hard in the side of his head. He was badly dazed, seeing stars and not fully aware that he had been knocked down. Fighting against the dizziness and nausea, he tried to make sense of what was happening and then to get up. Instantly the man was on him, kicking and punching him ferociously. Paul was getting badly hurt and was struggling to fend off the attack while simultaneously battling nausea and double vision. A kick to his face opened a deep cut under his left eye, which swelled up fast. Paul recalled, "I'm still dazed by the attack, bleeding badly. I'm flat on my back and my head is over the edge of the platform above the track. To my horror, I could see a tram pulling into the station. There was no question; I was now fighting for my life. I managed to land a few punches of my own and I could sense that he was beginning to tire. It must have been the adrenalin, but I started to get the upper hand and I pushed him back. It was still a hell of a fight to get him under control and properly restrain him until my backup arrived. When the tram driver gave his statement, he said that if he hadn't activated his emergency track brake when he did, I would have been decapitated."

Paul would find out later that his attacker had recently been released from Broadmoor secure Psychiatric Hospital, and that he was a former paratrooper who had been discharged from the army after bullying other soldiers. He was sentenced to three months in jail for the assault; a particularly lenient sentence considering the severity of the attack, especially as he would be eligible for release after just two months. Ironically, the first serious assault Paul suffered brought with it his first official complaint. The attacker alleged that he had used excessive force against him, but following an investigation that lasted a year, Paul was cleared of any wrongdoing. Regardless, the experience of how protracted and stressful it can be to be under investigation shocked him, even though he knew that he had done nothing wrong. However, the investigation was not to be his last.

More than twenty years later, Paul would receive another complaint, and this time it would change his life forever. It was on the 26th of January 2017, and he was driving a divisional van when he went to assist a colleague who had a male suspect detained. When Paul arrived at the scene, his colleague had the man sitting in the back of his police car and the door was open. The man in the car was belligerent and aggressive and took an instant dislike to Paul. He was under arrest for being drunk and disorderly and Paul's van was needed to take him to a police station to be booked in. Paul's colleague went to handcuff the man so that he could be safely moved into the prisoner cage. At once the man's aggression ramped up, and he pushed his way out of the car and began to resist violently. With his colleague restraining one arm, Paul reached for the other. As soon as he did this, the man snorted and cleared his nose: "From experience I knew that he was going to spit at us." The officers were able to pin the man against the car and prevent him from spitting at them by holding back his head. The man appeared to calm down and it seemed that he was ready to comply. As such, the officers stepped back and allowed him to stand up while they finished handcuffing him. The man turned to Paul, looked him in the eye, smiled, and spat a huge globule of phlegm directly into his face so that it entered his eye, nose, and mouth. He then resisted the officers as they fought to get him into the van.

"With my colleague following, I drove the male to Southwick Police Station. Throughout the journey the prisoner was shouting, swearing, and making threats that he was going to kill me or bite me." At the custody station, Paul opened the outer rear doors of the van and could see the prisoner through the inner Perspex door. The man was lying on his back with his feet towards the door. As Paul opened the inner cage door to get him out, he heard the man clearing his throat again as the man kicked out towards him with his right foot. To protect himself, Paul caught the prisoner's leg and pulled him from the van. With the prisoner now on the ground, he rolled him onto his front, preventing him from kicking and spitting at him or his colleague any more. He then escorted the prisoner into the airlock-style entrance corridor of the custody area where the prisoner immediately tried to throw himself face first onto the paved floor. To prevent him from injuring himself, Paul twisted and caught him, and held him up. In doing so he ended up supporting the man's dead weight and exacerbating a back injury he had sustained back in the mid-1990s.

He was injured after he had responded to an emergency assistance call from an officer who was dealing with a domestic incident. "I arrived to find my colleague laid flat on his back and a male above pinning him down and repeatedly punching him. The officer was totally unable to defend himself. I literally had to grab the offender by the scruff of his neck and the belt of his trousers to lift him and pull him away from the officer. I injured my lower spine, which has been a recurring problem throughout the rest of my career. At the time the doctors thought that I had displaced some discs. I then had to have eighteen months of physio until something suddenly cracked, and it felt like my back was okay. Unfortunately, over the years my back has popped out a couple of times, and when it does I am in agony. When it does happen, I'm not able to work on the front line as I can barely move, and I'm forced onto light duties until it improves."

Moments later, the prisoner threw himself to the floor of the custody office for a second time, and he and Paul stumbled, ending up in a messy heap. Despite being in agony, Paul managed to get him back up and transfer him to the holding cell. As he tried to lower the prisoner to the floor, he was unable to bear the weight of the struggling man any longer and he fell a short distance, hitting his chin on the floor and causing a three-centimetre cut. The custody sergeant then ordered the officers to take the man to hospital until somebody could be found to come and relieve them. This was a poor decision as Paul was in a great deal of pain and the man continued to be aggressive and combative which put Paul at risk as he would have struggled to defend himself. Once they were relieved, they were ordered to return to the police station and report to the duty inspector who informed them that, due to the injury the prisoner had sustained it was being treated as an "adverse custody incident". This meant an automatic referral to the Independent Police Complaints Commission (IPCC). It is worth noting that at no time did anyone ask Paul about the injury that he had sustained.

The following day, Paul was in so much pain that he was forced to report sick; however, within two hours the shift inspector and a sergeant arrived at his home and informed him that, due to the IPCC investigation, he was being removed from front-line policing and was expected to report to an office-based role the following Monday. He was warned that if he did not attend work for any reason, he would have to contact the superintendent immediately and that any absence or continued sick leave would need to be preauthorised by her. Paul had known that the incident would be investigated as the prisoner had sustained an injury and proper accountability was essential. However, everything suddenly seemed to have been blown out of all proportion.

Nevertheless, he accepted the instructions and although Monday should have been a scheduled rest day, reported to work. He was placed in a back office, twelve miles from his usual place of work and isolated from his team. Although the staff were welcoming and pleasant, there wasn't an actual job for him to do, so he filled his time making everyone's tea, and photocopying and laminating documents. With so much free time on his hands, he inevitably began to ruminate about the situation that he was in. Despite knowing that he had done nothing wrong he felt that the inquiry was escalating out of control. Therefore, he decided to contact the Police Federation for the assistance of a fed rep. The man assigned to him was an officer he had known for over twenty years and with whom he had a rapport, something which made him feel a little better.

Then on the 10th of February 2017, Paul was visited at work by the lead investigator for the IPCC. The investigator had brought along a colleague; however, Paul was not introduced to her and was left in the dark about who she was and what she did. "They had travelled 110 miles just to serve me with papers that I had used excessive force." Being a fair and practical man, he said, "The prisoner needed stitches, and as I was responsible for his welfare at the time, I knew an investigation was warranted. If people get hurt, it needs to be investigated to confirm that everyone acted properly."

He was stunned to receive a separate letter stating that "as well as an alleged breach of the professional standards of behaviour, there is an indication that you may have committed a Criminal Act of Assault". It was alleged that the prisoner had been lying face down in the van and Paul had simply dragged him out without any regard for his safety. This was manifestly different to the reality. Paul could not understand why he was still under investigation let alone the fact that they were talking about criminal charges. All the investigator needed to do was view CCTV footage from the custody and the body-worn camera that Paul's colleague was wearing, both of which recorded audio. It would have proven without any doubt that he had acted entirely professionally and that there had been no assault.

Paul was interviewed for over three hours on the 24th of February. "I explained everything to them in minute detail. I explained my rationale, my mood, my thinking, and my tactics." Only after that did they let him see the CCTV from the custody block. This did not include the audio recording.

"They seemed to be following the theory that I had lost control and had deliberately assaulted the prisoner in retribution for him spitting on me. They were suggesting that he may not have even been conscious and that he had been fully compliant. I explained that the two incidents were over thirty minutes apart and I provided them with the details of a witness (a member of the public) who would be able to verify my demeanour. To this day, the IPCC have never even spoken to this person."

Although the CCTV had been silent it had confirmed everything that Paul had told the interviewers. The only issue was that the footage of the van needed to be enhanced as it was unclear. It was totally unprofessional that this had not been done before the interview. Instead, they informed him that they would now prepare a prosecution file and forward it to the CPS requesting that he be charged with a criminal offence. He left the interview exhausted and dumbfounded. How could they justify trying to have him charged when the only evidence they had produced so far proved that there was no case to answer?

Five months later, Paul was still working in a back office. However, he was at home when he took a phone call from a different fed rep, late one Friday night. "I went upstairs into my bedroom and sat on the bed to talk to him. I remember his exact words: 'The CPS have made the frankly inexplicable decision to charge you with two counts of assault.' I was absolutely flabbergasted, but most of all, I was frightened; no, it was more than that I was completely terrified!"

The following week he received a summons instructing him to attend Peterlee Magistrates' Court on the 18th of July 2017. He had been charged with a Section 39 assault (essentially, an assault resulting in no injury) and a Section 47 assault (where the injury is of a low level). At the magistrates' court hearing Paul elected for a jury trial and the case was transferred to Teesside Crown Court.

The Section 39 assault charge followed the man being pulled from the police van by Paul. As previously stated, he had done so to defend himself from being kicked and spat on. It is important to be aware that the law allows anyone to use reasonable force to defend themselves from an assault. Furthermore, self-defence can be pre-emptive providing that the force is reasonable in the circumstances. As such, in this case there was clearly no assault.

The Section 47 assault charge was in relation to the suspect falling and sustaining an injury. Again, it has been shown that at the time the suspect was resisting and struggling, and as such the subsequent fall was clearly an accident. Remember that, had the suspect complied and not attempted to assault Paul, he would not have sustained an injury at all.

The fact that Paul was charged here emphasises a serious double standard in the way in which decisions are made in these circumstances, particularly if the victim is a police officer.

About eight years before this incident, Paul and a colleague had been patrolling a local Metro tram system when they had encountered two aggressive young men swearing and shouting abuse. It was obvious that other passengers were intimidated by their behaviour. The officers tried to calm the men down; however, they increased the level of their aggression, leaving Paul and his colleague with no option but to arrest them and remove them from the tram at the next stop. As soon as they moved in to make the arrest, both men resisted violently. While Paul was struggling with one, the rocking tram switched tracks and his knee was twisted badly, to the point of dislocation. The pain was overwhelming. However, digging deep, he held on to the man until the tram reached its stop. Once they were on the platform and with the prisoners finally secure, Paul pulled up his trouser leg to discover that his kneecap was now at the side of his leg. His knee has never fully recovered from this incident. When it came to charging the men, the CPS had refused to charge Paul's prisoner with assault, as they stated that Paul's injury was sustained during the struggle. Therefore, by the same standard there was no assault as the prisoner sustained his injury in very similar circumstances.

Preparing for the trial was the most difficult thing that Paul had ever done. "I made sure that I put plans in place. I wanted my wife to know all my passwords and where to find important paperwork. I was conscious that, if I was convicted, my salary would be gone. To ensure that we had a little breathing space, I wanted my wife to sell my car. There were times I was so low that I considered everything from running away to suicide. I just couldn't bear the impact me in prison would have on my family financially and emotionally. The anxiety and stress were compounded as the IPCC continued to stall and not disclose evidence to my barrister. We did not have the CCTV and audio files for the body camera footage. On two occasions when the audio file was sent it was on an encrypted disc that couldn't be accessed."

When Paul and his barrister did finally get a working copy of the body camera, they were able to zoom in and see that the prisoner was indeed lying on his back with his feet towards the door and when the footage was slowed down you could see that the prisoner had kicked out towards Paul. However, the IPCC would still not provide a usable copy of the audio. Nonetheless, it was incomprehensible that the CPS were still pushing forward with a prosecution when the evidence clearly proved there was no case to answer.

Unfortunately, too many officers are prosecuted when the threshold is barely met, and they are frequently perceived to be guilty until proven innocent. The media play a massive role in this, through sensationalist headlines and edited "clickbait" videos purporting to show abuse and injustice. This narrative feeds a frenzy of hatred and suspicion against the police. This was also a factor in Paul's case, and he was tried by the media as well as the court. On the eve of the trial the BBC headline declared, "PC Paul McVeigh assaulted man after being spat on. while the *Guernsey Press* claimed, "Officer threw handcuffed suspect face down on cell floor after being spat at". Paul said, "I was on the local TV news each night of the trial, and I made the newspapers as far away as Belfast and Cornwall, as well as the *Daily Mail*. The worst one was the *Shields Gazette*, which is my local paper, where my picture and the story were plastered on the front page." The *Gazette* is a popular local paper; therefore, Paul's friends and neighbours would read a slanted version of the truth. He is aware that there are still people who believe that there is "no smoke without fire" and that his reputation has been permanently damaged.

When it came to the first hearing in court, the judge appeared to be bewildered that the prosecution had still not produced either a summary of the evidence or a substantial allegation against Paul. The judge was scathing when he said, "I note that there is no MG5 (summary of evidence) contained on the file of evidence, so I looked over the injured party's statement, and to my surprise saw that this did not contain an actual allegation either." He was visibly annoyed by this, and Paul became optimistic that this might mean that the case would be discontinued.

The trial opened on Wednesday the 21st of February 2018, just a few days short of a year since Paul had been interviewed by the IPCC. It began with the prosecution setting out their "evidence" against Paul, which was weak to say the least. However, this did not stop the sensationalism and reporting bias. On the 22nd *The Northern Echo* published the headline "A police officer was caught on CCTV dropping a suspect face first and from a height onto the floor of his cell, a court has heard". The first sentence of the story read, "PC Paul McVeigh, 48, twice attacked [name removed], who he had brought in on suspicion of being drunk and disorderly". Although the media were assuming and reporting Paul's guilt there was still a trial to be heard.

The IPCC, now rebranded as the Independent Office for Police Conduct (IOPC), were still holding back on disclosing evidence. On the second day of the trial, they finally produced a copy of the audio recordings from the custody block. Incredibly, these were once again encrypted and so could not be listened to. This put Paul and his barrister in a very difficult position, either they apply for a mistrial, or they continue without a piece of crucial evidence that would disprove the IOPC's narrative that Paul had been angry and had acted while under the influence of a "red mist".

By this point, he just wanted the nightmare to end, so they proceeded without access to that evidence. The jury were shown the CCTV and body camera footage, however, without the audio the jury would never hear the prisoner's provocation and aggression and how calmly and professionally Paul had managed it. Proceeding without the evidence was an incredibly bold move.

Paul gave evidence on the last day. Although terrified, he remained professional and courteous. The prosecution barrister started her cross-examination by implying that Paul had a bad temper, suggesting that on the day in question he had experienced a red mist and she spent some time trying to provoke a reaction from him, before giving up on the strategy. Finally, Judge Simon Bourne-Arton QC summed up the case and the court broke for lunch. Paul was aware that when they returned to court the judge would discharge the jury so that they could make their deliberations. However, he had not expected the jury to return with a verdict just nineteen minutes later. Time seemed to stand still as he stood in the dock, waiting to hear what the foreperson had to say. In the end all he remembers are the words "*Not guilty! On both counts.*" He was overwhelmed by relief and joy as he left the court with his wife and legal team around him.

Later that day, after a couple of beers, Paul sat down to catch up on the news. As he'd expected, there was a story about his acquittal; however, his euphoria was crushed when it was reported that the IOPC now planned to hold a disciplinary hearing. "My future with Northumbria Police was uncertain. I could still lose my job and pension. I still think that it is unforgivable that I found out about the disciplinary hearing by seeing it on the news." So, after more than a year of stress and anxiety, nothing had changed, except that the threat of going to prison was no longer a prospect.

Paul was still unable to return to front-line policing, and remained hidden in a back office. It was as if being exonerated by a jury of his peers meant nothing. Indeed, that exoneration was now clouded with innuendo and suspicion. Despite knowing that there would be a disciplinary hearing, it would be months before Paul received any official notification of it. "While all of this was going on behind the scenes, I was left in no man's land again." The PSD arranged to serve him with the papers in person. "I was told, off the record, that I should be prepared to lose my job, so I started applying for work elsewhere."

Eventually, as part of the disclosure of the disciplinary hearing, Paul was given an accessible copy of the audio recording from the custody suite. Hearing it for the first time, he was very emotional. "I remember hearing the prisoner's maniacal laugh, and me speaking in my usual tone and without any heightened emotion. I couldn't believe that I had been denied this essential piece of evidence in court. Particularly as the prosecution had alleged that I was angry and the prisoner was subdued, or even unconscious.

The disciplinary hearing began on Tuesday 2nd of October 2018, with Paul facing five allegations based on the disciplinary code. These are detailed below:

1. Use of force: "Forcibly removed the prisoner from a police van, whilst he was handcuffed to the rear, by dragging him out of the van by his leg, you used unreasonable force."
2. Use of force: "Dropped a prisoner face first onto the floor of a holding cell when he was handcuffed to the rear. By dropping the prisoner, who was handcuffed to the rear, face first onto the floor you used unreasonable force."
3. Authority, respect, and courtesy: "Failed to take the appropriate care of a prisoner who was under your control, by forcibly

dragging him out of a police van, when he was handcuffed to the rear, and then dropping the same prisoner face first onto the floor of a holding cell whilst he was handcuffed to the rear. By failing to take appropriate care of a prisoner under your control, you failed to carry out your role and responsibilities in a diligent and professional manner."

4. Authority, respect, and courtesy: "Acted without proportionate self-control and tolerance by forcibly dragging a prisoner, who was handcuffed to the rear, out of a police van and then dropped the same prisoner face first onto the floor of a holding cell, whilst he remained handcuffed to the rear."

5. Discreditable conduct: "Forcibly dragged a prisoner, who was handcuffed to the rear, out of a police van, and then dropped the same prisoner face first onto the floor of a holding cell, whilst he remained handcuffed to the rear. By acting as you did towards this prisoner you behaved in a manner which brought discredit to Northumbria Police, and you undermined the public's confidence in the police service."

The facts of the original incident had been stretched to hit as many categories of the code of conduct as possible. Not only are they poorly set out, but they are also clearly presented as evidence of Paul's guilt. The facts are accurate, but only to a point. Yes, the prisoner was pulled from the van while handcuffed; however, these allegations ignore the fact that Paul was acting in self-defence as he did not want to be kicked or spat on again. It is also true that the prisoner was handcuffed when he was "dropped" onto the holding cell's floor. Again, though, they fail to put the action into context, in that Paul had injured his back whilst trying to control the struggling prisoner, and that he had done everything possible to carefully set the prisoner onto the floor. He was only dropped as Paul was in too much pain to bear the struggling man's weight any longer.

The facts were presented in this way as the hearing was not bound by the criminal burden of proof, which states that a person can only be found guilty if the prosecution prove "beyond all reasonable doubt" that they have committed the alleged offence. Instead, the misconduct hearing was bound by the civil standard of proof, "if on the balance of probabilities" you think somebody might be guilty. Finally, the hearing essentially went against the double jeopardy principle in law, which states that a person cannot be tried twice for the same offence(s) without further evidence of their guilt being uncovered. This was not the case for Paul.

Of the hearing itself, Paul said, "The prosecuting barrister went after me hard, much harder, even, than they had done at the Crown Court, because there was no risk that the jury might feel sorry for me for being treated unfairly. The gloves were well and truly off. The hearing took place over two days. It was like déjà vu, only this time the prosecution also had the benefit of knowing exactly what my defence would be from the trial." They attacked me from several different directions, with allegations that overlapped and contradicted each other. They had every angle covered. I told the truth and corrected the misleading evidence and the misquoting of my interview. The panel retired to consider their verdict over lunch on the second day. The result was *not proven*! On all five counts! I was absolutely delighted. I had been completely vindicated."

The IOPC, however, was still not done with him and began to discuss a judicial review to overturn the decision of the hearing. Triple jeopardy? It was a horrendous situation for Paul to be in. How many times did he need to be exonerated before they would stop persecuting him? If a member of the public had been prosecuted in this way, there is little doubt that they would likely be able to sue for a malicious prosecution. Paul spoke to the Police Federation, who informed him that there was no mechanism to fund a defence against a judicial review, and that, if it came to it, he would need to find the money himself. "They say that you cannot put a price on justice, but it seems that a judicial review can be very one-sided, unless you have very deep pockets," he remarked.

Fortunately for him, the federation and even the PSD pushed back hard against the suggestion of a judicial review and eventually the IOPC gave up on the idea. "I returned to work the following Monday. I didn't go back to response policing as I was posted to the wanted persons unit and then into the IS&T department, where I stayed until I retired in June 2020. I have never made an arrest or put my hands on another prisoner since."

If there is one positive outcome from Paul's terrible experience, it is that Northumbria Police introduced spit hoods for front-line officers, citing that they could be used as an alternative to force when defending against a spitting suspect. Paul's case was specifically considered as part of the decision, and as the training rolled out, he was proud to be one of the first to take part in it. It must be remembered that spitting on someone is a horrendous assault; moreover, when spit enters a person's mouth and/ or eyes there is a very real risk of contracting several horrible diseases which Paul was extremely lucky to avoid.

During his career Paul had been assaulted dozens of times. "I have been punched, kicked, bitten, headbutted and spat on. I have come close to being decapitated, as well as being threatened with a knife and a dog. I have had a wheelie bin thrown at me, and have been run over by a car. I made more than two thousand arrests and I have investigated thousands of crimes. I have done everything that I can to protect people and prevent crime."

During his career Paul served with the Territorial Support Group (TSG) the equivalent of GMP's TAU. In this role he played a part in policing many high-profile events including the London riots in 2011 and the 2012 Olympics. "I have also protected Her Majesty the Queen, Prince Philip, Prince Charles, Prince Andrew, the Prime Minister Tony Blair and President George W Bush as well as numerous other VIPs."

Of the many incidents and crimes that Paul dealt with, one stands out for him, and that is the murder of Laura Kane, who was nine years old when she was abducted and raped by a friend of her mother's. The child's body was found days later, under the floorboards in the offender's house. It was an exceptionally hot summer that year, and her body was decomposed. Although she was fully clothed, her underwear was missing. The offender claimed that she had hit her head while they were "play-fighting" and he had panicked and hidden the body. That is, until Paul and his team were carrying out a fingertip search in the area where the suspect usually walked his dog. "I spotted what I thought was a ping-pong ball, I checked it and it was girls' underwear tightly screwed up." Which, when forensically examined, contained her blood and her murderer's DNA. Had Paul not been such a competent officer, an evil paedophile could have escaped justice, instead, he was jailed.

Paul also recalled, "Following the shooting of my colleague, PC David Rathband, in 2010, I was on the manhunt for the gunman." PC Rathband had been sitting in a liveried police car when a gunman on the run for wounding his former girlfriend and killing her new partner with a shotgun cowardly crept up to the car and shot the officer through the car window. Twelve minutes before, he had called the police emergency number, declaring war on the police; an action hauntingly similar to the murder of PCs Fiona Bone and Nicola Hughes in September 2012. Paul was involved in the earlier stages of the manhunt, looking for the gunman at addresses in Newcastle, and then in the investigation in Northumberland and searching for evidence after the conclusion of the incident. PC Rathband had lost his sight after being shot in the face by a man whose only motive was a petty hatred of the police. Heroically, he created the Blue Lamp Foundation, a charity supporting members from all the emergency services when they are injured. Sadly, PC Rathband lost his own fight and died by suicide on the 29th of February 2012. However, his legacy now helps many people to put their lives back together. When the man who spat at Paul was sentenced, Paul was awarded a pitiful £50 in compensation, which is a disgrace. Nevertheless, the money was donated to the Blue Lamp Foundation where it could do some good.

I will leave the last few words of this chapter to Paul: "Policing is like constantly carrying a heavy weight: the weight of stress and the weight of responsibility. Complaints are part of the job; they are expected. Nobody likes being arrested and they are a good way to muddy the water in a trial. If one of them gathers momentum it really drags you down. Mine had the momentum of a freight train, and it took me to the lowest point of my life. For ages afterwards, I still couldn't shake free from the feeling that I was still under threat. The day I retired I had a Skype call with the chief constable, who I had known back when he was a detective. He thanked me for my service and told me that I deserved a happy retirement. Literally from that moment, life began to lift, a little at a time. A year later, I'm a completely different person. Life is now good. I will never underestimate the importance of the support of my wife, Joanna, who held me together when I wanted to fall apart."

TRIAL BY THE MEDIA

I make no apologies for the police, and I fully accept that on occasion officers have committed the very worst of crimes. There are those who harbour abhorrent racist and sexist views, and on the rare occasion these officers have treated both the public and their colleagues atrociously. However, these people make up only a tiny minority of the service at large. It should also be noted that nobody despises bad officers more than good officers. Indeed, there is no organisation that works harder to identify and root out these despicable people. In fact, in the fervour to remove bad officers, officers who are completely innocent are frequently dragged through deeply harmful and traumatic investigations.

Through the stories of Richard, Jonathan, and 'Anna' it's clear that police forces aggressively investigate their staff when they make a mistake. The officers were treated abhorrently, and in these cases the forces gave absolutely no consideration to the underlying mitigating circumstances. However, Paul was tried and found guilty by the media before he was tried in front of a jury of his peers in a court of law. They immediately reported a narrative of him being a violent power-obsessed man, and as the trial progressed maintained that view even in the face of other evidence. This reporting could have swayed the jury and caused an innocent man to be convicted. Unfortunately, where the police are concerned this is the norm rather than the exception.

To demonstrate my point, I will present a couple of examples from the second half of 2021. On the 30th of July the *Daily Mail* published a clickbait video captioned "Shocking moment police officer punches man in the face during arrest". The video shows a man violently resisting arrest and assaulting an officer before he is punched. The headline to the story stated, "Police chiefs defend officer who was filmed punching a handcuffed man in the face after drink-driving arrest saying the suspect was FIRST to attack cops who did not use 'excessive' force". Again, there is the inherent accusation of wrongdoing and of closing ranks.

In another example on the 29th of September, *The Independent* published a video captioned "A cop fly-kicked a 15-year-old girl to the ground, a shocking video has shown". In the footage the girl is seen trying to free another female who is already violently resisting arrest. The girl assaults the arresting officer and then another when police backup arrived. An officer then delivers a leg strike bringing her violence to an end and she too is arrested. Although the video isn't easy to watch; it has to be acknowledged that officers are entitled to use reasonable force in self-defence. Again, the headline doesn't represent the reality of the incident.

I cannot make any further comment on either incident as frankly I do not know all the facts and I am unaware of any intelligence or information that the officers involved may have known about. An officer's decision to use force is theirs alone and will be based on their experience, knowledge, and perception of risk. As such, it is wholly irresponsible for the media to attach a biased and anti-police narrative on what can often be just a few seconds of edited footage.

For every negative interaction with the police there are thousands of others in which officers arrest the most heinous criminals, save people's lives, and safeguard children and victims of domestic violence. Yet these successes are rarely celebrated. It is little wonder, therefore, that 78% of the officers responding to the police Pay and Morale Survey of 2021 said that the police are not respected by the public. It is little wonder when the public are so influenced by this slanted and sensationalised reporting. The examples above push the narrative of police brutality.

In a final example from the 8th of May 2020, Sky News reported "Man tasered by police in front of child at petrol station as incident referred to watchdog". The *Liverpool Echo*'s headline was "Video showing police tasering man as child cries 'daddy' prompts calls for review" whilst the *Daily Mail* reported, "Shocking moment police Taser 'drink' driver in 'unnecessary force' in front of his screaming child at petrol station as Labour's Andy Burnham calls for urgent probe and police refer incident to IOPC." To gain some political capital, Andy Burnham, the Mayor of Greater Manchester, issued the following statement:

"On Friday morning (8 May 2020), a video was brought to my attention of a police incident at a petrol station in Greater Manchester involving two police officers, a man, a child and the use of a taser. I was concerned about what I saw and immediately asked GMP to look into it and provide me with an explanation of what had happened.

"From what I have been told, it would appear that the officers were right to apprehend the individual who was putting his child and others at risk by his actions. He has subsequently been charged. But it is not at all clear that the level of force used in this instance, particularly in front of a child, was proportionate or justified and that is why I have asked for an urgent and independent review to be carried out."

Although the Mayor heavily suggests that the police used excessive force, the MP for Gorton, Afzal Khan, clearly stated the accusation when he tweeted, "Very alarming to see @gmpolice using such undue force and in front of a small child. I hope this will be looked into as a matter of urgency @CCIanHopkins @DeputyMayorofGM @AndyBurnhamGM @NickTorfaen". At that point, GMP had already voluntarily referred the incident to the IOPC for investigation.

So, what were the facts? The incident took place at eleven o'clock at night when the child should have been safely tucked up in bed. Instead, he was in the car with his father, who was driving under the influence. The father was charged with drink driving, driving at seventy-two miles per hour in a thirty-mile-per-hour zone, failing to stop for the police, two counts of resisting a constable in the course of their duties, and failing to provide a breath sample. As the country was in lockdown due to the coronavirus, he was also charged with unnecessary travel.

At trial he pleaded guilty and was given an obscenely light sentence of an eighteen-month conditional discharge, he was banned from driving for just fifty-six days, and fined £420. In mitigation his solicitor stated, "He has accepted he lied to the police at the scene, and he didn't engage with the breath test [but] does that give the police the right to deploy a FIREARM?" The use of this word is extremely inflammatory, and to me evokes the shootings of black suspects by cops in the US as well as a cynical attempt to shift blame for what happened from the offender to the police. It's often the case that the media will report cases of police misconduct or brutality, however, it is only when the reader goes beyond the headline will they discover that the incident took place abroad, and not in the UK.

In this case the press went further than just implying that the police are violent but also motivated by racism. On the 9th of May *The Daily Mirror* headline read "Vigil at petrol station where police

Tasered dad in front of his screaming son." The article reported that anti-racism campaigners had staged a protest at the venue. Further the newspaper also stated, "Mobile phone footage widely shared on social media showed an altercation on Wednesday night between a black man and two white police officers." I can see no other reason to bring up the races of those involved except to stoke up racial tension.

Ultimately, after more than a year under investigation by the IOPC, the two officers in this case were vindicated when the IOPC stated that their actions were in line with police policies, and they should not face disciplinary action. It went further stipulating that racism had NOT been a factor in the incident. It is outrageous that these officers and their force were depicted as racist and violent when they were simply doing their job and protecting the public.

PC "SARAH"
(WEST COUNTRY, ENGLAND)

As the person concerned wishes to remain anonymous, I will use the name "Sarah" throughout this chapter.

For Sarah, it was never in doubt that she would join the police. To her, it was a vocation, a choice that went all the way back to primary school. Her interest was piqued when she was eight and accidentally left her Nintendo at the dental surgery, returning to collect it, she realised that it had been stolen. She said, "I remember my mum taking me to the local police station to report it, and then a police officer coming to our house a few days later to give it back to me. I thought it would be amazing to be able to help people when they needed it."

The only question then was *when* she would join. She delayed doing so for a few years to get some life experience that she knew would make her an even better officer. So, after completing her degree in environmental management, she took a job with the county council as a rural transport adviser. The role involved writing up policies and bidding for funding which would be vital in connecting rural communities with larger towns and cities.

In December 2000, aged twenty-six, she couldn't avoid the calling any longer and joined the police. Policing turned out to be everything she had hoped for and more. After her basic training she was posted to Wadebridge Police Station in rural Cornwall. "My team were fantastic and there was a great camaraderie between us all. Although we were single-crewed (working alone) in the day, we were doubled up for night shifts. My usual partner, known to all as 'Badger' was a brilliant guy. I couldn't have asked for anyone better."

Sarah is a spiritual and empathetic woman with a gregarious and compassionate personality, which made her particularly good at dealing with victims of crime and vulnerable people. It is no wonder, then, that she put herself forward to be trained as a sexual offences liaison officer (SOLO). This meant that she would be called out from home to assist in any allegations of rape or serious sexual assault. Her role was to support the victim throughout the investigation and any subsequent trial.

With just over a year under her belt, Sarah was deployed to a serious road traffic accident in which a nine-year-old girl had tragically lost her life. Soon after the cordons went up, the girl's parents and little brother arrived at the scene. The parents were devastated and kept asking, "She's dead, isn't she?" Although Sarah suspected that they were right, without official confirmation by a medic she couldn't say anything. She was therefore forced to continue reassuring them for hours before she was tasked with taking the family home and, when the time came, breaking the awful news to them.

Once she had completed her probation, she moved onto a proactive public order and drug squad. She was excited about the new role: "It was also good to escape some of the exposure to trauma." Work on the squad proved to be great fun as she enjoyed developing intelligence and locking up drug dealers, executing warrants and taking part in public order operations. Although, as a SOLO officer she was still regularly called out to assist victims of sexual violence. However, everything changed on the 21st of

December 2002 when the team were tasked with investigating the death of a baby boy.

Harley Rogers was just nine months old when he died. His death was particularly harrowing due to the callous indifference shown by his killer. The boy's mother was in a relationship with a new partner who detested the baby as he looked like his natural father; so much so that he had punched the infant in the face. The dreadful violence escalated when the boyfriend's fifteen-year-old brother swung the baby like "a baseball or cricket bat", hitting Harley's head against a door just to shut it. The heartless thug then hit Harley's head against a chimney breast in the same manner. The mother was unaware of the assault as Harley's hair hid any physical injury; however, she had been concerned enough to take him to the hospital. There, over a period of thirty-six hours, Harley slowly succumbed to his injuries and died.

The investigation and the evidence the officers gathered took a personal toll on Sarah, especially when she had to go up to London to collect Harley's brain from the coroner. The brain, in a bucket of formaldehyde, rested between her legs in the footwell of a car on the journey back to Cornwall. "I didn't join the squad to investigate murders.' If I had wanted to do that then I would have joined the CID." A few years later when she was pregnant, she had a recurring nightmare in which her baby fell from an upstairs window, crashing onto the road below, where the skull would crack open, exposing the baby's brain. As the years progressed the team would again be pulled away from their drug squad duties to investigate another murder.

By 2005 the psychological effects of experiencing repeated trauma and death, coupled with her suffering a miscarriage, were beginning to have an impact on Sarah. She was acutely aware too, that her colleagues were noticing that she wasn't quite herself as they made comments like "Where's your mojo gone?" or "We want the old Sarah back." It came to a head one evening when she was on duty with her sergeant. They were sitting in a car when a member of the public came over and began to criticise their choice of parking spot. They were not parked illegally and were there for a specific purpose. Though usually easy-going and good at talking to people, Sarah reacted to his petty ranting and told him where to get off. She had not been aggressive or particularly rude, but her response was unlike her. Once the man had gone her sergeant turned to her and said, "You're not very well, are you, Sarah?" Although the sergeant was correct, and the statement and his intentions were good the words were demoralising and frustrating and they hit Sarah hard. She knew as well as anyone that her "mojo" was missing and she desperately wanted to be her old self again, but that is not an easy thing to achieve.

The next day she reported sick and took a few weeks off with stress, hoping to recharge her batteries. She tried to convince herself that some rest would do the trick and she would be able to get back to normal. But on returning to work she still had a feeling of disassociation, and although her sergeant had acknowledged that she had not been well, nothing was put into place to ease her back into work. Instead, she was just expected to pick up where she had left off.

In 2007, after five years on the drug squad, Sarah was looking for a role in which she could make more of a difference in people's lives, and took up a new position on a neighbourhood team. Working closely with people suited her down to the ground and she became involved in several projects, including raising awareness around food poverty. A key part of this was teaching response officers to identify shoplifters who were stealing out of necessity, and refer them to other agencies who could help them. She also established a scheme whereby people in need could collect food vouchers from the police station. There will always be those who criticise this type of work and claim that offenders should be locked up regardless of their circumstances. However, the first principle of policing is to prevent crime, not to respond to it. A scheme like this prevents hard-working retailers from being victims of crime, supports those in need, and frees up police officers to deal with more urgent matters.

As a devout Christian, Sarah would occasionally attend church services in uniform. This allowed her to engage people who had little or no contact with the police, in the same way that pop-up stands in supermarkets or community centres do. Speaking to the public in this way can often achieve great results through the intelligence that is gained, but more importantly, the neighbourhood teams can then directly target the issues that are causing people the most concern.

Another important issue the team got involved in was Speed Watch, through which local people were able to work with the police to tackle drivers speeding dangerously through their towns and villages. All said, the work done by Sarah and her colleagues saw them win Neighbourhood Team of the Year on two separate occasions.

As she was driven to help people as much as possible, Sarah undertook training to become a lost person search manager (LPSM). In that role, she was responsible for coordinating and planning searches for high-risk missing people. A high-risk missing person is anyone likely to come to substantial harm if they are not located quickly. Unfortunately, that often includes suicidal people. It is exhilarating to find someone safe and well; however, often that does not happen. "With each search I felt the burden of the anxiety and trauma involved, and it became all-consuming." Inevitably, this constant pressure took a further toll on Sarah.

In 2011 she attended a large house split into bedsits. One of the residents – an alcoholic – had taken an overdose. "I knew it was going to be horrible, so I told the PCSO who was with me to wait outside for an ambulance, as there was no reason that he should have to face what was happening. I found the man collapsed in his room; he was alone. As I started resuscitation, the man took an agonal breath." Bravely, she continued CPR on the body until the paramedics arrived and the man was transferred to the air ambulance. Although he had probably already died, Sarah had fought desperately to maintain life until the professionals took over, it has been known to bring people back from the brink and she desperately hoped that that would be the case.

Later in the year, a teenage boy on her beat area was strangled to death by the scarf that he was wearing. In memory of him, Sarah, and a PCSO arranged for kids to complete a graffiti memorial in the local park. At the time there had been no coroner's inquest into the boy's death; therefore, when Sarah wrote her regular newsletter which would be distributed to the area's residents, she deliberately avoided speculation. Having created a draft of the newsletter, she went on rest days, intending to finish it off when she returned to work.

However, she returned to find that her sergeant had finished the newsletter and distributed it. Not only that, but she had made changes stating that the boy had died by suicide. "I was livid, and I ended up having a huge stand-up row with her, as what she had done was so unprofessional and deeply insensitive. The argument ended when the sergeant broke down crying." Although Sarah felt sympathy for her, she added, "I had built up a good relationship with the family and I was worried about their reaction to the news. I didn't want them to suffer any more pain than they already had. Fortunately, they agreed that it had been a mistake and accepted my apologies." Incidentally, the coroner ruled the death as misadventure, not suicide.

Sarah had been deeply affected by the death and trauma that she had witnessed over the years, and was struggling to cope with the heavy burden she was carrying. Taking matters into her own hands, she contacted occupational health. She was seen by the force psychiatrist, who diagnosed PTSD, and the force organised some treatment for her, allowing her time off work to attend the sessions. Initially the treatment was successful, and she felt much better. Despite her diagnosis this became a missed opportunity to safeguard her, there was no consideration around changing her role. As such she continued to work as an LPSM, and thus to face death and destruction on a regular basis, which continued to grind her down.

There would be further incidents that would severely impact Sarah's mental health. In one case an elderly vicar went missing after leaving a suicide note. Sarah was on the clifftops above a beach when she spotted the man's body in the sea below. While she was trying to organise a lifeboat crew to recover the body, the tide came in and the body was swept away and wasn't discovered for several days. Throughout those days Sarah was extremely anxious about the body ever being recovered and returned to the vicar's family. There wasn't a day while he was missing that she wasn't consumed with worry. More than six years later, she can't walk near the cliffs around Cornwall without vividly reliving the incident. But she doesn't want to ruin those walks for her loved ones, and so must endure the memory alone.

In 2014 Sarah moved from her neighbourhood role back to response policing and also trained to be a TRIM facilitator, again putting others' needs above her own. This involved contacting colleagues who had been involved in traumatic incidents and offering support and advice to help them work through the difficult incidents they had dealt with. She says that officers who did take up the support were worried about the stigma of doing so and would want to meet somewhere private or a local coffee shop. The role was hard work; however, she found it very rewarding.

Also, in 2014 she began training to become a priest within the Church of England. She had a vision of not only shining her light as an officer, but also providing the service of a police chaplain. She was heavily involved with the Christian Police Association, which had already provided her with a prominent faith role in the police. In fact, in 2017, alongside the chief constable, she led the force's Memorial Day service at their headquarters. Often, she relied on prayer to aid her psychologically when dealing with incidents.

As a search coordinator she was increasingly being pulled away from her normal duties to coordinate searches. By 2017 she was being called out as often as three times a week. The force was also struggling with a crippling shortage of staff. To address this, they relied on "removal orders" to move officers from their normal duties to another station where there was a shortage. Officer safety is a real concern in this type of situation as a transplanted officer doesn't have the local knowledge that they do at their normal station. Such as who is likely to assault the police, who is particularly dangerous, or even which areas it's unwise to go alone. Although policing is a hazardous occupation, this knowledge at least mitigates some risk. Furthermore, as the officer has been moved because of shortages, they will be conscious that their backup could be a considerable distance away, adding another layer of stress and anxiety.

In July 2017 Sarah was sent to attend to a woman who had climbed over the railing on the Tamar Bridge. On arrival she found the twenty-two-year-old woman sitting on scaffolding on the outside of the bridge. Sarah and another officer who had just arrived tried to build a rapport with the young woman, and to encourage her to return to the safer side of the bridge. Sarah was desperate to help the young woman and prevent her from harming herself. They kept her talking for twenty minutes, and hoped that they might be getting through to her. However, despite their efforts, she shuffled forward and, tragically, fell to her death on the road below. Sarah describes the sound of the young woman impacting the road as being "like a shotgun going off". This, too, is a memory she relives all the time.

As the police were present at the time of the woman's death, there was a mandatory referral to the IPCC for investigation. A referral to the IPCC can cause extreme anxiety as it is well known that their investigations are often protracted (in many cases, they have continued for several years), which can lead innocent officers to worry that they are going to be unfairly prosecuted.

Just two months later, and while still under investigation, Sarah was covering for staff shortages in another part of the force when she attended another suicidal woman. This time the woman was behind a closed bedroom door. She had taken an overdose, had a noose around her neck, and was armed with a knife. Sarah began negotiating with the woman, with the constant, nagging fear that, if the woman died, it would lead to another IPCC investigation. However, following two and a half hours of careful negotiation, Sarah, assisted by a paramedic, finally managed to talk the woman out of suicide and into accepting medical treatment. When the woman came out of the room she was taken to hospital by ambulance.

Unfortunately, this incident broke Sarah. She was exhausted and under investigation, and the burden became too much for her to bear. The following day she reported sick, and she would never return to work as a police officer again.

Two weeks later she went to see her doctor, knowing that she couldn't articulate what was going on in her head. She had made notes on her phone, which she handed to him in the consulting room. The notes explained just how compelled she was to self-harm, including a notion she had about driving her car into the path of another vehicle. Her emotional pain was so intense that she needed to release it by feeling physical pain; she wanted to be seriously injured. She recognised that she could be killed; however, her attitude was "if that happened, then it happened". It's clear that she was in a horrendous place because, despite being so compassionate and loving, she had not even considered, at least at a conscious level, that her actions could also affect somebody else. Subconsciously, though, she is so hardwired to protect other people that, if things had come to that point, she would never have been able to carry it through. The doctor expressed his deep concern for her and immediately prescribed medication.

Towards the end of September, and after a couple of weeks of the medication, Sarah felt that it was making her emotionally numb. She felt detached from herself and her family. She was so despondent that she drove out to the moors and took an overdose of medication. Just before she set out walking, her doctor called to check on her progress. Sarah broke down and told him what she had done, and he convinced her to go to the police station. Sarah did what he asked, but parked up at the ambulance station around the corner. A PCSO, and later an inspector whom she had worked with for a long time, came out to speak to her. She said that the inspector was amazing in the way in which he handled her and got her to hospital, where she was immediately put on a drip so that the medication could be flushed out of her.

This had not been a suicide attempt she was just so overwhelmed by psychological and emotional pain, the only way to soothe that pain was to cause herself physical pain. In a similar vein, many police officers suffering with stress, anxiety or burnout will abuse alcohol to numb their feelings. Ultimately these impulses play a significant role in self-destruction.

In October Sarah headed to the beach with a knife in her pocket and took another overdose. She desperately wanted to walk out into the sea, but she knew that she needed help, so she phoned 999. The officers who arrived were both friends of hers: one was her sergeant from her time on the drug squad and the other was somebody she had done her police training with. Pleading with Sarah, the PC approached her and tried to comfort her with a hug. The anguish and desperation that Sarah was feeling were suddenly too much and she took the knife and stabbed herself in the stomach, causing a three-inch-deep wound. "I deeply regret what I did and the effect that it would have had on the officer. She was so brave and only wanted to help me." Sarah was detained and sectioned under the Mental Health Act. The power allows the police to compel a person to be taken to a place of safety where they can be psychologically assessed. However, due to the stab wound and her need for urgent treatment, Sarah wasn't taken to hospital under police guard as she had to be airlifted off the beach.

In hospital, she was again placed on a drip and her wound was stitched up. Luckily, she had not hit any organs or caused any permanent damage. The following morning, she was assessed and allowed to go home. Her husband took six weeks off work to care for her. She said, "Basically, he had to babysit me. I became very good at hiding my illness, so soon things began to get back to normal, although, inside I was an absolute mess."

In the early hours of New Year's Day 2018 she managed to sneak out of the house with a bag she had prepared. "I had all the things that I would need in a crisis: I had stockpiled medication, tobacco, alcohol, and a knife. It was comforting to know that it would be there if I ever needed to flee." She walked to an abandoned cattle market where she once again stabbed herself in the belly and took an overdose. This wound was not as deep as the first and again she was lucky not to cause any permanent damage. She was again sectioned by the police, taken to hospital, and again the hospital released her the next day.

By February or March, Sarah's self-harming had evolved to include a dressing-gown cord which she would knot and throw over the top of a door, so that when the door closed the knot would prevent the cord from pulling through the space between the door and its frame. "I would lower my weight so that the noose took the strain, and stay there until just before I blacked out. Again, it was not a suicide attempt: I used dressing-gown cords because they would snap if I got it wrong and did black out." Sadly, Sarah had more than one near-death experience while using a noose, but despite it being such a high-risk behaviour she continued just for some psychological respite. She recalls one incident when she lost consciousness. "As I regained consciousness, I felt a presence: it was like there were three or four people working on me; I felt they were trying to save me. It was an ethereal experience: the figures looked like people although they didn't have faces. I wasn't scared, and would say that it was a comfortable experience. It was my faith; I just knew that God was with me, and his light and love were enveloping me."

In June 2018 Sarah was retired from the police on the grounds of ill health, and since then she has worked extremely hard to recover her mental health. There is no cure for PTSD, but through therapy the impact of the symptoms can be addressed and minimised so that the sufferer can learn to manage the condition. Sarah has done that and is no longer self-harming; indeed, her medication has been reduced. She told me recently that she even has her "creative mojo back", as she has started to draw again. Although she collects her work in a book, other drawings have been turned into unique and personal cards for her friends and family.

Although Sarah is concentrating on her own health, she is still committed to helping people, and has recently completed a mental health first aid (MHFA) course and is considering volunteering in the future. "My husband has been an absolute rock despite all that I have put him through; he motivates me to be well and I don't want to let him down. I have amazing children and am enjoying my time with them." Although she doesn't know what the future holds, she wants to take it slowly and enjoy her life, currently she has no plans to return to formal training as a priest.

In conclusion, Sarah offers these words: "Being a police officer has been a calling for me from an incredibly young age, and something I knew I had to do. Despite the horrific incidents I have witnessed and the torment I have been through, I wouldn't change anything for the world. It has been an immense privilege to serve my Queen and country as a member of the force. I have touched so many people's lives, being there during their darkest times, and been blessed with helping them through it. I also feel so blessed to have worked with so many amazing colleagues who are friends for life. I'm very philosophical and know everything happens for a reason – the trauma I have been through, and the darkest depths of my PTSD, have all been for a higher good. The very essence of me has remained throughout all these events, and continues to shine its light stronger and brighter than ever. I know that I will help so many other people because of what I have been through, and that is a tremendous blessing."

PC DARREN ATKINS
(METROPOLITAN POLICE)

Growing up in a small Cheshire town, Darren was impatient to finish school and get some life experience. His happiest childhood memories were of long days spent at the beach, where he would stare out to sea and wonder where the ships slowly crossing the horizon were headed. He imagined the different cultures and people that the crew would encounter. He had always wanted a job in which he would be personally challenged, offered adventure, and, most importantly, would help or benefit others. It is no surprise, then, that he wanted to pursue a career in the Royal Navy. He applied as soon as he left school; however, unfortunately his dream would remain unfulfilled as he was rejected due to childhood asthma.

At a loss as to what to do with his future, he decided that he didn't want to carry on studying as he had found school "mind-numbingly boring". While he considered his options, he took a job with a major supermarket chain and quickly became a fresh food manager. Within a couple of years, he was settled in a relationship, earning good money and on the fast track to management. However, he was not fulfilled, and still wanted more out of life. He said, "I needed to do something that mattered; something that had a real meaning and purpose to it. I didn't want to just sit around and get a pay cheque." Influenced by the stories his mother had told him about her time as a special constable, he began to consider policing. It was a career that represented everything he had wanted out of the navy. There was no doubt that his innate compassion and empathy would make him a very good officer and he joined the Metropolitan Police in late February 2005, aged twenty-two.

"The training I received was great. I was in a fabulous intake and my classmates were brilliant. I made some lifelong friends during that time. Everything was going great until we got towards the end of our training, when my intake was sent to the G8 conference in Gleneagles in Scotland. We ended up being used to protect the buildings in the inner cordon. We had only been there several days when I saw the news of the 7th of July suicide bombings back in London. In no time we were packed up and shipped back to the police training centre in Hendon. Once there, the intake was split up and given different jobs. I was tasked with doing security patrols around the training centre, others were taking witness statements in relation to what had happened, while the last group ended up guarding the temporary mortuary. It was definitely an unusual way to start our careers.

"When we did eventually pass out, I was posted to the borough of Islington, a very wealthy area of North London, but with pockets of extreme deprivation. It was an amazing place to work, and I had the absolute pleasure of working with extremely professional police officers. My sergeant was brilliant: he was firm, funny, and he ensured that I got the best possible start to my career." Once Darren had settled in London and found a place to live, his partner moved down to join him. She would later get a job at the police call centre.

For all new officers there comes a defining moment when they realise that they are doing the job for real. For Darren it came when he and some colleagues were called to a fight outside an Irish bar. "We arrived to find two pumped-up, angry drunks fighting with a doorman. We got stuck in and had a decent roll around, trying to get the drunks restrained. It wasn't easy as they had taken drugs and seemed to have a crazy amount of strength. I spoke to the doorman afterwards and found out he was a former Iranian soldier who still had a bullet lodged in his leg. I found the whole thing very exciting; I loved the thought that we had taken down violent criminals. I was in the Big Smoke now and life had got way more interesting than in leafy Cheshire." As his career progressed, he came to realise the naivety of this statement, as he dealt with extremely violent offenders and the carnage that they left in their wake.

Following the arrest of the men outside the bar, Darren was staggered by how poorly the criminal justice system performs. On contacting the CPS and passing them the case papers, he anticipated that the men would be charged with violent disorder (a serious public order offence) amongst others. The violent disorder charge was appropriate based on the disgusting level of violence the men had used against the bouncer. However, the CPS refused and charged them with the lesser offences of affray (essentially, a straightforward fight) and actual bodily harm (or ABH, which is a less serious assault), as well as criminal damage and racially aggravated public order offences. Darren was disappointed by the lesser charges which minimised the gravity of the incident; however, he was still hopeful that the victim would achieve some justice in court.

Attending court on the day of the trial, Darren reported to the prosecutor, who was overwhelmed by all the cases that had to be tried that day. "I couldn't believe it; the defence had had months to concoct the story and the prosecutor hadn't even read the file." In the end the prosecutor just made a deal with the defence: they dropped the criminal damages completely and reduced the affray to a lower public order offence that basically meant that the offenders had acted in a threatening manner. In the end the two men got a slap on the wrist and a fine of a couple of hundred pounds, and the victim, who had been through a horrible experience, was just forgotten. It was just so wrong, but little did Darren know at the time that it would become the norm. It is so hard to get the CPS to even charge in the first place, and when they do charge, they often reduce the charges and ignore the victim because any court disposal counts as a win. Darren added, "I must have made over a thousand arrests in my career, and I always worked hard to ensure the victims received justice; however, there were so many times I felt guilty, like in some way I had let the victim down because the jury had found the defendant not guilty, even when the evidence clearly proved their guilt. It became so wearing to look a victim in the eye and say how sorry I was that the court system had failed them so badly."

Although disheartened by the court experience, his enthusiasm for the job pushed him to work harder. "Islington was a busy patch, and we had a lot of the same sort of crime. Street robberies were very common, with wealthy residents being targeted for their watches and other luxury items including cars. It was great fun as we would get involved in some interesting jobs. There were a lot of bars in the area so there were also a lot of alcohol-related punch-ups to keep us busy, but hey, it was exactly what I wanted to be doing." There were days that we would be pulled off response to do other tasks. With the threat of terrorism so high we would regularly do a shift on the 'bomb car' where we were given a list of high-value targets. We would drive around continually, visiting them through the shift. The only incidents that we were able to attend were suspicious packages. I remember one at the church on Tottenham Court Road: they had received a package full of wires, batteries, and CDs. In the end I virtually shut down Central London while we waited for the bomb squad to arrive and deal with it. It was amazing to see, and really reminded you that the threat was real. In the end, the package was harmless. It had been posted from an address in Germany and, as it turned out, there was another from the address in close succession. That was investigated by other officers, so I never found out what the motivation for it was."

Darren had completed his street duties course without dealing with a sudden death. Unfortunately, this is one of the more unpleasant rites of passage that no officer can escape forever. Having never seen a dead body before, Darren was understandably worried about how he would react, particularly as he would be under the scrutiny of his colleagues. When the day came, he was on patrol with his sergeant when the report came in. As policy dictates that sergeants are required to attend all sudden deaths on their shift to confirm that there are no suspicious circumstances, Darren quickly realised that he was going to be dealing with the incident. "As soon as I got out of the car, I was overwhelmed by the most horrendous smell I could ever imagine. It was a smell that turned my stomach. Incredibly, the smell just got stronger as I climbed the stairs to the second-floor apartment. Once I got there, I could see that there were hundreds of flies buzzing around the window. I entered the apartment and saw an officer standing over the body of a man lying face down on a mattress. The body was horrifically bloated. My sergeant instructed me to turn the body over and check for anything that might suggest an unnatural death. I took hold of the deceased man's arms and began to roll him. I could barely cope with the stench, just talking about it means I can smell it now. Anyway, it took everything I had not to throw up. However, once I turned the body over, I saw that it was seriously decomposed and riddled with maggots. That image is etched on my mind; it's something I'm never going to forget." This was the first traumatic incident of his career. He wanted to talk about it, but he also didn't want to bring it home. As there was nothing else that he could do, he pushed the memory deep into his subconscious.

It didn't take long for Darren to realise that policing involved a lot more than just locking up bad guys. In addition, the police are required to deal with everything that other agencies like the NHS and social services have no resources to deal with, chiefly these incidents involve people with serious mental health conditions which make them a danger to the public, as well as those who regularly abscond from hospital or secure units. "I remember being given a job of finding and returning a woman who had absconded from a secure mental health hospital. My colleague and I went to her home address. When we got there the front door was open, so we went inside. We found her sitting on a mattress on the floor. As soon as I started to speak to her, she pulled a large kitchen knife from under the mattress and said, 'This is for you, you cunts!' Fortunately, we acted quickly and were able to disarm her. Still, it was a serious struggle to get her back to the hospital. It was my first real encounter with a blade, and one I wasn't eager to repeat."

With his two years of probation completed, Darren transferred to the neighbouring borough of Camden, as it was bigger and far busier and gave him the chance to gain more experience. Moreover, the shift pattern in Islington had been horrendous and meant that he rarely saw his partner. Now their shifts were more closely aligned. However, "It is fair to say that Camden borough was where I experienced the best and worst times of my police career. There were so many stabbings, most of which went unreported in the press. At times we were having two, maybe three stabbings every set of shifts, a set of shifts will usually consist of four to five days."

He had not been in his new post long before he himself responded to a stabbing. "I was on duty working with a probationer, and when we arrived, we found a twenty-one-year-old victim on the floor behind a block of flats. The man was drenched from head to toe in blood, which had also pooled around him on the ground. When I first got to him, he was still bleeding profusely and gasping for breath. I attempted to stem the bleeding by putting pressure on his wounds, but he had been stabbed fifteen times and there were just too many holes. It was a nightmare; I didn't have the skillset that would help me save his life. All I could do was hold him and try to reassure him as he died in my arms." Later, back at the police station when Darren was in the shower, scrubbing off the dead man's blood, he promised himself that he would get more advanced first-aid training, one way or another.

"I managed to get onto a public order first aid course, where I was taught advanced first-aid skills, equivalent to what an emergency technician would receive when they joined the ambulance service. It has absolutely helped me to save lives during the rest of my career. I genuinely believe that all police officers should be trained to this standard, as too many of us turn up at jobs where someone passes away, and we shouldn't have to live with the question of whether we could have done a better job. I now know from personal experience just how horrendous it was to have someone die in my arms.

"To be able to save someone's life is the most incredible feeling in the world. It happened when I was called to yet another stabbing. We arrived to find a man in his seventies slumped against the wall outside a block of flats. When I checked, the man had a twelve-inch kitchen knife sticking out of his side. It looked like he had been cut across the stomach, as his intestines were hanging out of the wound. While I was guiding my probationer colleague on how to stem the blood flow, the victim told us that the man responsible for stabbing him was a neighbour who was still inside the block of flats. I immediately called for backup as we would be in a very dangerous position should the offender come outside and decide to attack us too. It wasn't something that we could dwell on as we just had to get on with our jobs. As it was, the ambulance wouldn't come to the scene while the knifeman still posed a danger. It felt like we were on our own for an eternity, but it was probably only about ten minutes before other officers had the offender arrested.

I later learned that if we hadn't done what we had the man would have died."

In the aftermath of the stabbing, it was discovered that the suspect had been detained for a mental health assessment the night before, as he was hearing voices telling him to kill his neighbour. However, again he was able to just walk out of the hospital. Darren was commended for saving the victim's life, and would be commended for saving a second life when he attended a domestic stabbing outside a taxi office. In that case he had to push his fingers into the wound to stop the bleeding. The recognition for his good work was appreciated; however, it did nothing to stave off the trauma and the impact that these incidents were beginning to have on him, he continued to box them away inside his head. What Darren really needed was for someone to recognise that these incidents were seriously affecting his mental health. If someone had asked him how he was, he would have had the opportunity to ask for the help that he so needed. Unfortunately, nobody did, and he was put off by the stigma of declaring a mental health issue and the fact that people would suddenly treat him differently and he feared losing the respect that he had worked so hard to earn.

Over recent years, the number of people stabbed in London has reached epidemic proportions, tragically many of the victims and perpetrators are just children, and far too many are dying alone in the streets. "The number of stabbings was increasing and soon we had six or seven every set of shifts." This is what faced just one team of officers working from one police station, take a moment to imagine how much knife crime there is across London and the other major cities of the UK, put into context in this way the scale of the problem is terrifying.

"With my extra training I went to every incident I could where I might be able to help. Although it was mostly stabbings, I also went to car accidents and people self-harming. I was compelled to do whatever I could. As I was a tutor constable, I was often paired with probationers. I always believed that I had a duty of care for their welfare, so I was able to comfort and support them with an imaginary arm around their shoulder, and try to reduce the trauma they experienced. It is almost impossible, though, when you turn up at a scene to find someone barely alive after half his head has been caved in with a claw hammer."

As time progressed, Darren found it harder and harder to keep pushing down the memories that haunted him. "I had tried to harden up and keep things down; it was making me feel numb. I tried to keep it all behind a door in my mind, but I was concerned that the time would come when I wouldn't be able to close that door anymore. I just didn't want it to affect my family, but how do you go home smelling of death when you have a new baby in the house without it having an effect? Every shift seemed to bring another type of horror and violence. I didn't like that it was becoming second nature to sit near a suicide victim and casually write up my notes.

"In the end I would spend more time at work than at home. I didn't really regret that because I knew what I was doing was helping people. My friends and colleagues were my rock; we relied on each other. After work we would go to the pub. Sometimes we would vent to each other; most of the time we would just get smashed. I could see other people who were broken; we were drinking to forget and sleep just so that we could get up the next day and do it all over again. Whatever happened, though, we were always there to support each other. I needed that time because I felt that I was protecting my family by not bringing home all the shit that I dealt with at work.

"One time I was out with a probationer in the early hours of the morning, we were just off Camden High Street. The street was full of bars, and it was just about kicking-out time, so it was very busy. We were then alerted to a man who was bleeding heavily from a large open wound that went down his forearm to his wrist.

I managed to clear out the wound and contain the bleeding. While we waited for an ambulance somebody came up screaming about a man with a knife. I had to leave my colleague with the casualty and ran in the direction they pointed. I called for backup as I made my way there, then I was suddenly confronted by a man brandishing a combat knife. It was like something Rambo used in the movies. I shouted to him to drop the knife and he replied, "You're getting it, you fucking pig." I swung my baton and hit him hard, knocking him off balance. I was lucky as just then my colleagues arrived, and we managed to detain and handcuff him. Without them I would have been in deep shit. Crouching down to seize the eight-inch blade, the reality of how close it had come to me possibly losing my life hit me hard. I now had two children at home, and they could have so easily woken up later that morning without a father."

A couple of years later, Darren was attending a call for emergency assistance at Euston Railway Station, where a police officer was being strangled by a drunken man. "As I was running down the ramp towards the platform, my utility belt gave way and, as I bent to try and catch it, I tripped and fell. I fell around seven to eight feet, landing on my back. I damaged two discs and a vertebra, and I spent seventeen months struggling to walk and I knew that my career had, in that one incident, come to an end. I was medically retired on 1st of April 2015.

"It was very hard to lose the career that I had dedicated my life to. When I signed up, I had no way of knowing just how little the training I received would prepare me for the job. I had a close bond with my colleagues and have made some lifelong friends. However, I was left with horrible, haunting memories that I couldn't control. This is down to the lack of mental health support offered by the job. It led me to be diagnosed with CPTSD and depression. In the end, all the memories that I had boxed away flooded out and overwhelmed me so much that the only way that I could see a way forward was to take my own life.

"Although I had two children at home who I adored, the mental and physical pain was all-consuming, and I couldn't see any other option. I took all the boxes of diazepam and amitriptyline I had and then drove to the top of Dunstable Downs. I took every tablet I had. The last thing I remember of that night was two police officers arriving at the side of my car. I tried to speak to them, but I passed out.

"The next time I woke up was in the intensive care unit at Luton and Dunstable Hospital. When I had recovered enough, I was assessed psychologically and given the choice: either my dad travelled the two hundred miles down to collect me, or they would section me in a secure hospital. It was the lowest point of my life when I called him, saying, 'Dad, I am in a bit of trouble, and I have done something silly. I need your help could you please come and pick me up and bring me home? I will explain more when you get here.' He said, 'Whatever it is, it doesn't matter. If you want to talk, I am here to listen.' Although I have been made to feel ashamed by some, my dad understood."

In conclusion, Darren said, "I have spent the last six years coming to terms with my mental health. I cry from time to time, I have some serious ups and downs, and I struggle a lot when I relapse. However, I now lead a happy and quiet life in the Shropshire hills with a new partner and three other children, we have what can be described as a small petting zoo in the back garden. I'm getting my life on track, and I have spent the last three years studying to become a counsellor. I figure there isn't much that I haven't experienced personally, and that experience means I now have a deeper level of empathy for others. It is another way of making that positive difference to people. It's what I signed up to do all those years ago. I would like to be able to work with members of the emergency services so that I can help them before they end up in the position that I did. It is a terrible fact that only once during my ten years in the job did somebody ask me if I was okay."

Darren and Sarah are not the exception to the rule, as up and down the country officers are pushed to the very limit of their mental and physical capabilities, only to then be forced out of the service on ill-health retirement. When they are retired, there is no fanfare, no retirement party, one day they're a police officer and the next they're not. The career to which they have given so much simply fizzles out like a damp squib.

POLICE SUICIDE

It's estimated that a serving police officer in the UK completes suicide every two weeks, and unfortunately this is a long-standing problem. In researching this subject, I began in 2003 as it was the year that I joined. My research goes as far as 2019 as there is no data available for 2020 and beyond. Incredibly, **383** serving officers died in that period.

The death of a police officer is a tragic event, yet police work is very dangerous, and officers do lose their lives while doing their duty. However, safeguarding and protecting officers' well-being can prevent suicide. It is scandalous that between 2005 and 2019 more serving officers have died by suicide than in a duty-related death. *Fifteen consecutive years.*[1]

This, however, only represents the tip of the iceberg as it does not include officers like Nicola Hughes and Fiona Bone's colleague Mark, as he had left the service at the time of his death. This is because the coroner will record the deceased's present occupation on the death certificate, and it is from this information that the Office of National Statistics (ONS) compiles its data. As such, official figures also do not account for the suicides of special constables as their primary occupation is recorded on their death certificate. Finally, the ONS doesn't have an occupation category for police staff, other than PCSOs.

It would be reasonable to assume that each force would keep a record of suicide among their officers and staff. In December 2018 I submitted Freedom of Information (FOI) requests to every force in the UK, asking if they kept a record of their officers who complete suicide. Five forces did not respond and just six of the other forty-three kept a record. In June 2021, Sam Smith of "Green Ribbon Policing" submitted the same FOI request, albeit limited to just the forty-three forces in England and Wales. In the intervening three years just three other forces had begun to keep a record. The consensus seems to be to ignore the problem, because acknowledging it would force those in charge to do something about it, and that is going to be extremely expensive. But money should always come a distant second to saving lives and preventing the devastation that follows in the wake of a death.

I do not contend that every police suicide can be solely attributed to the officer's work. After all there will be numerous contributing factors. However, the forces have a duty of care to their officers and police staff, and should ensure their welfare. There are several factors where suicidal ideation is increased, for example:

- Officers who are under or believe they are under investigation. Tragically a colleague whom I admired greatly took his life because he wrongly believed that he was under investigation
- Officers who are or believe they are being forced out of the service
- Trauma
- Stress
- Bullying
- Burnout
- Stigma

In any of these cases the risk is escalated if the officer is self-medicating with alcohol or drugs (prescription drugs included).

PC SAM SMITH

(HERTFORDSHIRE CONSTABULARY)

For Sam, becoming a police officer was a long-held dream. On leaving school it was the only thing that he had ever wanted to do. Although he would achieve his dream, it would prove to be bittersweet, as it came to an end after a little over two and a half years' service.

By the time Sam was old enough to apply to join the police, forces around the country were beginning to feel the effects of public spending cuts, and recruitment was frozen. While he waited for his opportunity, Sam worked in various sales and account management roles, and at nineteen he joined Hertfordshire Constabulary as a special constable intending to gain experience that would aid him when the police resumed recruiting.

He said, "I always had ambitions to join, and dreamed of being a police officer until retirement." Although special constables have the same powers as regular constables, the training is basic at best. Typically, a special constable will undergo weekend and evening training over several weeks, whereas a regular constable will undertake up to four months of residential training before being posted to a police station. Special constables usually make up for the shortfall in their training by working with experienced colleagues to develop their knowledge and skills. Unusually, following his training Sam was posted to a regular response team. "I was very keen and passionate about wanting to do well in policing. It didn't take long before that enthusiasm was sucked out of me! The team that I worked with showed a complete disinterest in the special constables; they clearly didn't see me as an equal and they didn't spend any time trying to teach or develop me. After a year I took the extremely hard decision to resign and wait until I could join as a fully fledged police officer."

As it turned out, three years later the recruitment freeze had still not been lifted, so Sam decided to join the army and serve four years, after which he should be able to apply. Accepted into the Tank Regiment at twenty-four, he threw himself into training and enjoyed the discipline and camaraderie of being a soldier. Unfortunately, a shoulder injury in the gym saw him pulled out of training and sent to the recovery unit. "After several weeks on the unit I was called to the sergeant major's office. I remember his words so clearly: 'I'm sorry to tell you this, but you're going to be discharged from the army. Apparently, your injury could take years to properly heal, and that means you're not able to complete the training at this time'." Sam was able to take some solace from the fact that he had received excellent training reports, and that the door was open for him to return to the army when he was fully recovered. "I had to come to terms with the very real possibility that a career in sales might end up being my destiny."

However, the police soon started to recruit again, though he now needed to complete a Level 3 Certificate in "Knowledge of Policing" before he could apply. To achieve the certificate applicants were required to complete 250 hours of training, and the cost of the course, £850, was payable by the candidate. Further, successfully completing the certificate did not guarantee that the candidate would be recruited. Nonetheless, determined to fulfil his ambition, Sam signed up paying for it with money that he had saved while in the army.

To support himself he took on another sales role. "I found the job dull and uninspiring; I had never liked sales as I never had any sense of moral achievement, but I had to do it to pay my way."

His hard work and determination finally paid off when in March 2017 he joined Hertfordshire Constabulary as a regular officer. He was now twenty-five years old. Shortly before he joined the police, Sam met Daisy, who was on a clinical placement and in her second year of a master's degree in forensic psychology. They shared an interest in policing, and they quickly became a couple. Daisy remembers how happy Sam was when he went to training school, and how he really enjoyed the training and met good friends.

Sam said, "My time at the training school went by so fast and I was suddenly policing the streets of St. Albans. I remember thinking, *How am I ever going to do this job? There is so much to learn!* But things just started to click. My team were amazing, we were like a family. It's hard to describe the bond we had. It was like nothing I'd ever had with previous colleagues. I remember being at a sudden death very early on in my career. The gentleman was badly decomposing into the floor and maggots were eating away at his face. The smell was one I will never forget; I could taste death in the air. A matter of months before, I'd been asking customers what colour font they wanted on their balloons. Nothing can prepare you for policing; it is a job like no other."

"I lived and breathed work and I barely had time for outside friends as I was working hours and hours of overtime. I constantly felt exhausted but there was something thrilling and exciting about it all. Policing is like a drug once you start doing it, you need more and more to satisfy your craving. In my career I would deal with a huge amount of death, violence, and tragedies. I became well known for writing up comprehensive reports for the coroner, so sudden deaths soon became my speciality, and I was sent to a lot of them. Being around rotting corpses and grieving families became normal to me. I have always been compassionate and very victim-focused, so I became an initial contact officer for serious sexual assaults and rapes. My working day was often filled with sadness and great trauma, but as a team we often overcame this with dark humour and often normalising extreme circumstances."

Daisy added, "In that first year it seemed to me that Sam was always at work; I had to get used to him still being at work hours after his shift should have finished. Then there were the endless training days; it seemed that he was always being made to work. I had noticed that he was different, though, I put it down to the fact that he was so tired all the time. I began to worry when he started talking in his sleep about bodies and paperwork. I could understand most of what he was saying, and it was as if he was at an incident."

Sam continued, "I remember noticing that my resilience had got worse, and I was finding it hard to tolerate some behaviours. I'd also become so hypervigilant that I found it hard to drive anywhere off duty, as I would notice everything that people were doing wrong, and it would fill me with rage and frustration. Daisy would tell me about the things I was talking about at night, but I have no memory of it. After about a year and a half I had completely changed as a person. I rarely went out in my free time, and everything revolved around policing. I know that Daisy was concerned about me, but I would get defensive whenever she brought it up, and would argue that that was just the way police officers are. It was like I was having an affair with policing, and she didn't get a look in.

"One day after work, something just snapped in my head, I don't know why. Yes, I had had a difficult shift, but it was nothing out of the ordinary. I was completely overwhelmed with the feeling that I just couldn't go back to work the next day. I phoned Daisy on the way home and told her that I couldn't do it anymore and I didn't know what to do about it. She suggested that I make an appointment to see the GP, and I got angry with her for even suggesting it. She had encouraged me to make an appointment a couple of times already, but I had always ended up cancelling them as I tried to convince myself that I was fine.

"When I got home, Daisy insisted that I took the next day off work and that I go and see the doctor. I tried to change her mind, arguing that I couldn't take time off because the team needed me, and anyway, I was just having a bit of a moment and I would be fine. Eventually, after some persuasion I agreed that I would speak to the doctor, but I had planned to go into work straight away afterwards.

"When I went to the doctor it surprised me that she had remembered that I had cancelled a previous appointment. I had never had a lot of experience with doctors, so I was reassured when she was kind to me and genuinely seemed to care. Still, I was cautious about what I'd said to her, as a good friend of mine had told me that if I ever disclosed a mental health problem then my career would be over. Nevertheless, she told me that I was very close to a breakdown, and she signed me off work for a month. I was completely overwhelmed by this news, and anxious about how my sergeant and team would react."

Daisy added, "When Sam came back from the doctor, he was completely shocked that she had signed him off work. To be honest, it was exactly what I had expected her to do. He was very unwell and needed some time away from policing. By this time, I also worked for Hertfordshire Constabulary, in a civilian staff role within the investigation management unit. As nobody from Sam's shift had contacted him while he was off work, other than to tell him to drop off his sick note, I began searching for contact details for the Employee Assistance Program (EAP). It proved almost impossible until I found out that the information was on a poster on the back of the toilet door. I don't know how anybody in need of help was supposed to find it. A couple of the police officers in my office gave me some advice, but what I found very strange was that these conversations were always whispered as nobody wanted to be seen talking about mental health. I remember that the only thing that I was asked was whether he was suicidal, and as he wasn't their attitude seemed to be *okay then, we'll just leave him to sort it out on his own.* There was no interest in taking proactive steps to help him recover."

Sam said, "I went back to work after a month on the sick, and it felt as if my team were distancing themselves from me. However, I only had a couple of weeks left with Hertfordshire Constabulary as I had been accepted as a transferee to Guernsey Police. Everything seemed to be fitting into place well, as Daisy managed to find a job as an assistant psychologist on the island. So, I just kept my head down and cleared any outstanding work that I could, and handed over everything else. I was very sad to leave Hertfordshire Constabulary in the way that I did, as I had put everything I had into the job. I had worked every hour that I could as I genuinely wanted to make a difference for the people who needed us, but in the end all my work and personal sacrifices were for nothing, and I felt totally unappreciated. I hoped that at least a new start and a slower pace of life in Guernsey would be just what I needed to get my life and career back on track."

The couple arrived on the island a few weeks before starting their new jobs, and reflecting on that time Sam said, "The weather was great and the scenery and beaches were beautiful, I guess it felt like a bit of a holiday. When I did get started, I had two weeks of training to get me up to speed with the differences in law and procedures. Again, it was all very laid-back, and I was feeling positive about the future."

At the end of the training, Sam joined his new team, who were working nights. "In Hertfordshire the level of demand was relentless; we would be constantly busy and under huge pressure, but in Guernsey it was the opposite and I found that the shifts dragged on, leaving me with too much time to think. On the first night we went to a domestic incident where a woman was causing problems. I was frustrated that the Guernsey officers kept giving her 'last warnings' when she had no intention of listening and carried on causing problems. As they weren't doing anything positive, I got frustrated and I stepped in and arrested her. I had not policed for two months; I was aware that I hadn't resolved the issues about what had caused me to go off sick in the first place. Then on the last night of the set we were dealing with an alcoholic. The stench was horrible, and suddenly I was right back to where I was two months before and I thought to myself, '*I just can't do this job anymore.*' I was at my wits' end, and I didn't know how I was going to mention it to Daisy, as we had dedicated everything to this fresh start. I reported sick and disclosed what had happened in Hertfordshire. My inspector was good and appeared to be very supportive, and promised that they would get me all the help that I needed to get better. She even disclosed her own struggles with mental health, and I felt reassured that things might turn out okay. While I was off sick, I had three one-hour counselling sessions through Guernsey's Employee Assistance Program while I was waiting for them to arrange the proper help.

"I had been off for a few weeks when a senior officer turned up at my home. He basically told me that I was on a six-month probationary period and that they had no intention of allowing me to get through it. Therefore, he suggested that I should resign. The rug had been pulled from under my feet, and I was devastated. My dream career was over, and I was being forced to resign. I was disappointed as my inspector had promised so much and it hadn't materialised. When I wrote my letter of resignation, I stated that I didn't want to leave the police and that they were forcing me to do it. I said that I had given everything I had to policing, and that I had been let down as I had never had the chance to have my mental health treated. I was proud to be a police officer, and I hoped that I had helped the people that I had met during my service.

"Along with losing my career, I also lost my work permit. Daisy didn't have one of her own and was working on mine, and now risked losing her job too. To make things even worse, we had signed a one-year lease for a house. We just didn't know what to do. Daisy's boss had offered to get her a permit, and we discussed the idea of her staying and me returning to Hertfordshire. In the end we both decided to come home; neither of us had jobs or a place to live, and we had had to sacrifice our security deposit to break the lease. So, in October 2019 we came home and ended up having to go back and live with our parents. Unfortunately, neither had the space for both of us and, as Covid was breaking, we were not able to see each other for months. I was twenty-eight and living with my parents again, and I couldn't get any help for my mental health because of the pandemic, so I just became very depressed as I couldn't find a job."

Although Sam was still devastated at losing his beloved career, he was also angry about being forced out of policing because of his mental health. He absolutely believes that, if the police had arranged appropriate treatment he would have recovered and been able to resume his career. Within weeks he harnessed that anger and committed himself to campaigning for a national standard that would ensure that any officer in any force would get help when they needed it. "I had been mulling ideas over in my mind and eventually came up with a plan of action and couldn't wait to share it with Daisy. We talked the plan through into the early hours of the morning. The first thing that I did was create an online petition calling for the introduction of a national standard for mental health support in policing. The petition was going very well, and I quickly had seven thousand signatures, but then Covid hit again, and the petition stopped growing. That said, it was useful evidence about the extent of poor treatment of mental health issues in policing, as hundreds of people had shared examples of their personal experiences.

"My other strategy was to go out to the forces and speak to the chief officers and the people responsible for well-being. Although most people were receptive to what I was saying and appeared to be enthusiastic about the idea to my face, in the end they never followed up on their promises. In one case I spoke to a superintendent who seemed to be very positive, but then he sent me a rude and condescending email telling me that there were no issues in his force and challenging me about what qualifications I had which supported what I was trying to achieve. I guess that he just didn't grasp that I was qualified to discuss the issue because of my lived experience." The reaction of the superintendent demonstrates why so many officers are let down when they need help. Frankly, it is easier to turn a blind eye to the issue, because as I have said before, once you recognise it, you then need to address it.

Sam and Daisy had been working hard to push the campaign forward, and decided to name it "Green Ribbon Policing". At the same time, they changed strategy and began to lobby the government to introduce a national standard for mental health. In doing this they also wanted the government to establish a legal framework obligating police forces to improve mental health provisions and training for their staff. It is a fact that early treatment is the best route to maintaining good mental health. Without that intervention, the cumulative exposure to trauma leads to officers reaching breaking point, at which stage resignation or medical retirement are the only ways forward. Sam said, "If it had not been for Daisy and her psychological insight I would have probably just pushed on and on. Who knows, I might have done ten years before I was completely and utterly destroyed and had absolutely nothing left."

In one of the many discussions that I have had while researching this book, I was told that recruits spend more time learning to march than they do learning about maintaining good mental health. I therefore sent an FOI request to the College of Policing, asking about coverage of mental health in officer training. In response I was told that it was up to the individual forces to decide what goes into their recruit training. I then submitted the same request to the Metropolitan Police, as they are the biggest force in the country. They disclosed that their officers have "a full day of training on wellbeing and resilience which covers support for themselves and their colleagues, including how to identify support organisations". They also have learning packages around mental health, although most relate to dealing with the public. As for marching, "at present the student officers spend five hours per day for a two-day period on teaching and practice relating to their passing out Parade".

As the regional training centres have now closed, it's down to each force to train their recruits. As such, mental health training may differ vastly around the country. Although I give credit to the Met for providing training in well-being and resilience, it's a concern that preparing for a passing out parade appears to be as important, if not a little more.

Sam said, "When I joined, I didn't receive any training around mental health and resilience; though things are beginning to improve slowly since I left. This is partly due to the influence of Green Ribbon Policing, although the focus on mental health still falls far short of that of physical health. In officer safety training, officers are taught how to protect themselves from a physical attack, so they should also be teaching them how to protect their mental health."

After their return to the mainland, Sam concluded, "Daisy was able to get a job first, although not as a psychologist; she took a job in customer services. It turned out to be a good move as she has now been promoted a couple of times and is an international business development specialist. It took me six months, but I got a job with Barnardo's, where I was working with children at risk of criminal and/or child sexual exploitation. However, the post was funded, and when I learned that it might be at risk, I got a job as a safeguarding lead at a specialist school for children with Autism. It is a high-pressure role, but it is also very rewarding."

CONCLUSION

Jonathan Nicholas titled his book *Who'd Be a Copper?* and this is an extremely important question. The officers featured in this book clearly wanted to serve and protect their communities from the criminal elements in our society. They are heroic, resilient, and committed to helping those in need, and they have given a huge part of themselves to that fight. They are not robots, as beneath the uniform they are wives and husbands, parents and children. They are scout leaders, football coaches and school governors. They are the fabric of our society, and hold the line between good and evil. Without the police there would be chaos and anarchy.

In July 2021, when the government announced that they were lifting the public sector pay freeze, the police were given a 0% pay rise, while the fire service received 1.5% and the NHS 3%. I accept that the rises offered to the other emergency services are far below what these employees deserve; however, by offering the police nothing at all, the government once again demonstrated the depth of the contempt with which they regard the service. Due to the pay freeze and real-term pay cuts, the police have seen their salary plummet by around 18% since 2010.

Then in 2012 the government forced through changes to public sector pensions from the more generous final salary pension to a career average scheme; a blatant act of age discrimination. Again, there are those who will say that the police pension was already very good. I accept that it is better than some other pension schemes; however, police officers pay a hefty 13.44% salary contribution, which is the highest in the public sector. Unlike the rest of the sector, the police are the only body who are unable to take any industrial action. The Police Federation, elected to represent the needs of the rank and file, did virtually nothing to fight the changes and vigorously refused to mount a legal challenge against the discrimination.

Instead, it was left to officers themselves to organise their colleagues and mount a legal challenge. In 2019 the Home Secretary finally conceded that the implantation of the pension changes was discriminatory. However, that decision was taken only after the Fire Brigades Union and court judges had taken their cases to the Court of Appeal and won. To date, the matter has not been resolved and no police officer knows what their pension will look like in the future or when they will be compensated for their financial loss.

We have one of the best police services in the world and it is crucial that that doesn't change. This will involve a great deal of commitment and investment by the government and police chiefs. Urgent and consistent interventions to improve the support offered around mental health are essential as is a strategy to prevent suicide among officers and other police staff. Every force must record the suicide of every member of staff, including special constables.

A national standard in mental health treatment is essential to ensure that everyone who needs help receives consistent support. Every officer needs to be trained in how to manage their own and their colleagues' mental health. Supervisors need extra training in how to assist and manage, so that they can offer support and refer the officer to others within the force who are properly trained to offer them the correct help.

Police officers, and indeed all the blue-light services, should have priority access to the NHS in the same way that the military have. It is abundantly clear that early, effective treatment, particularly around mental health, increases the likelihood of recovery. Conversely, not receiving early help whilst continuing to be exposed to trauma reduces the opportunity to recover, as the person will often become more unwell. The government and chief officers have a duty of care to their staff and cannot keep their heads in the sand any longer.

Between 2017 and 2021, 37.8% of medical retirements in the UK were attributed to mental health. I recognise that work is being done around the Police Covenant which has the potential to greatly improve the conditions under which our officers are working. However, to achieve that necessary aim, it needs to address a wide range of issues as well as being accountable. Oscar Kilo, the National Police Wellbeing Service, is doing some good work raising awareness and rolling out well-being dogs; however, that is nowhere near enough. Indeed, when Oscar Kilo visit stations in their well-being vans it is invariably on a weekday during office hours, which means that the officers who need the most help are least likely to have the time to visit them.

Violence against the police is now virtually out of control and the government must commit to ensuring that anyone who attacks a police officer is sentenced to prison. The CPS should not be bargaining with defence solicitors and downgrading the seriousness of an assault just to get a court win. There must be a deterrent to assaulting officers, it appears that criminals can assault the police almost with impunity, and that is evidenced in the large annual increases in assaults against the police year on year. If the guardians of society are not protected, then who will protect the public?

British police officers are weighed down by an unmanageable workload which is taking its toll. Our officers are burned out, stressed, and often extremely traumatised. Many of those who have shared their stories here turned to alcohol as a coping mechanism. In researching this book, I have spoken to hundreds of officers. I also created a survey concerning the mental health and welfare support available to officers, 850 responded, and they came from every police force in the UK. In all the respondents shared well over 1000 stories and examples relating to the lack of support they received. Therefore, I can assert without hesitation that alcohol abuse is a serious problem within the police. There needs to be a grown-up conversation around alcohol wherein officers who have a problem can safely ask for help and as long as they are actively engaging with support they will not be dealt with punitively, particularly as alcoholism is a significant factor in suicidal ideation. As things currently stand, officers are afraid to ask for help because they fear investigations by professional standards and that their careers will be destroyed.

When officers are investigated by professional standards they should expect to be treated fairly and the investigation to be dealt with in a timely manner. It is also unacceptable that officers are perceived to be guilty until proven innocent. Being under investigation is another factor in suicidal ideation, and is another area where proper support needs to be implemented. I accept that some officers under investigation are guilty; however, that shouldn't be a factor in their death. Indeed, suspects in police custody or under investigation are protected by reams of rights and entitlements and every effort is made to safeguard them.

Police numbers have been cut savagely due to the government slashing police budgets between 2010 and 2018. This resulted in the loss of 21,372 officers in England and Wales, which is in real term a loss of 15% and the lowest number of available officers since 1981. The cut to police numbers hit even harder as, during the same period, 25,000 civilian members of staff were also cut. Although the government committed to recruiting a further twenty thousand officers, there has been only a slight increase and there are still 10% fewer officers than there were in 2009.

Although forces around the country are once again recruiting, across England and Wales there is a serious problem with the retention of officers. Thirty-one of the forty-three forces in England and Wales responded to my Freedom of Information request asking what percentage of officers recruited between the 1st of January 2016 and the 31st of December 2021 had since resigned. The results were alarming and ranged from just 1.4% in North Wales Police to a staggering 56.4% of officers at Cheshire Constabulary, on average 12.4% of new police officers are leaving within five years. It should be acknowledged that a small number of these lost officers may have transferred to a different force; that said, this will have a negligible effect on the overall percentages. This creates a vicious cycle wherein huge amounts of money are spent on recruiting, training, and equipping officers, only for them to resign and the process be repeated.

There are many factors that underpin this issue, such as violence, stress, mental health problems, low morale, a high workload, and having to work far longer to receive a smaller pension, all of which play a part. As does salary. People assume that police officers are highly paid, this is untrue. An officer's salary is very close to that of a teacher; however, as the teacher's pension contribution is almost 6%, they will immediately have a higher take-home pay. I do not object to what teachers earn, indeed, like the police, they're not properly renumerated for what they do. But although teachers also work outside school (marking would be an example), they are not working alone in the early hours of the morning, they don't risk having their rest days cancelled, and they're not faced with the levels of violence and trauma that officers deal with daily. In the 2021 "Pay and Morale Survey" conducted by the Police Federation, 92% of respondents said that they are not compensated fairly for the stresses and strains of their job, and 86% that they are not compensated fairly for the hazards inherent in their job. Added to that, 73% said that they were worse off financially than they were a year ago. It is little wonder, therefore, that 47% of officers reported that a poor salary increased their intention to leave the service. Then there are the 14% of survey respondents who said that they are never or almost never able to cover their essential monthly costs.

As the cost of living and energy prices are now soaring, this will only get worse, especially if the government continues to grant the police lower annual pay increases than the rest of the public sector. The situation is already very serious, as reports from the Police Federation indicate that officers have been unable to heat their homes and are relying on food banks and welfare vouchers to feed their families. Andy Berry, the chair of the Devon and Cornwall Police Federation, said, "I know officers who have had to take their cars off the road to make their wages last, others who have left policing to earn more money elsewhere, and single mums struggling to make ends meet with an ever-increasing cost of childcare." Indeed, on the 13th of April 2022 Suffolk Police Federation shared the story of a 29-year-old mother-of-one who had resigned. The officer is reported to have said that handing in her notice was the hardest decision she has ever made but she found herself unable to pay for petrol at the end of the month due to the costs of childcare for her son. Most officers are not in the job for the money, as clearly there are far better-paid jobs outside of policing. They do it because they want to make a difference and protect the communities that they serve. That said, they will continue to leave the service if they can't afford to feed their families.

Despite all these hardships, the men and women who police our streets manage to hold the thin blue line. Theirs is a very difficult job in which decisions are made under a great amount of pressure, knowing that, if they make any mistake, that decision will be scrutinised by people who make their judgement from the warmth and comfort of an office. It is said that to err is human; however, the expectation is that the police must always get it right and to the satisfaction of all parties, and when they do they receive little gratitude for their efforts. It is an impossible task, yet every day they still turn up and put themselves out there while trying to do everything in their power to protect and serve the public and they do so with great courage, dignity, and integrity.

ENDNOTES

1. This information was established by comparing the number of suicides against the line of duty deaths recorded on the police memorial trust roll of honour.